BEDTIME STORYTELLING

Bedtime Storytelling

A Collection for Parents

Beatrys Lockie

Floris Books

For my grandchildren,
Fergus, Morna, Ena, Keira, Roscoe and Jamie

First published in 2010 by Floris Books
© 2010 Beatrys Lockie
Illustration page 17 © 2010 Alma Dowle

British Library CIP Data available
ISBN 978-086315-736-3
Printed in Great Britain
by Cromwell Press Group, Trowbridge

Contents

Telling Stories to Children

Why Tell Stories?

We all love stories. There are so many ways to tell a story: through music, dance, ballet, theatre, with puppets and directly to an audience.

Do you remember being told stories? When did it take place and where? On a parent's, grandparent's or friend's lap? Was it in bed, snugly tucked up before going to sleep: that wonderful space when all is done, before falling into a warm drowse? Or was it only in the holidays when there was time?

Not so many children nowadays have this great experience and yet it's an essential tool in their upbringing. For through stories one can create moods and feelings and gently lay down moral views without ramming them down children's throats. Stories are like food to them. If they don't get them at an early age, it's a great loss, never to be regained, which can even affect the child's subsequent emotional life.

Why do children not have stories told to them these days? The honest answer is that it takes time and trouble. What are we grown-ups doing with our time? Mostly working, as we must earn money. But here we should strike a balance between what is good and necessary for our children and what our materialistic society demands of us.

What is so special about telling stories? Well, you have two arms free to gesture as you tell the story — you can wipe a nose. But, above all, you have eye contact, which means you can observe and react to how the child feels. If necessary you can stop the story to solve the child's problem and then carry on again.

By contrast, when reading a book (a very good second best), your eyes are on the page and you cannot have such a close relationship with your listener. Nor can you easily hold a child or make gestures. But reading aloud is still better than leaving the child alone to listen to a tape while Mum or Dad gets on with things. First of all, the child is alone so there is no physical contact. Furthermore, who is this person telling the story? It's a disembodied voice. The child can't interrupt to ask a question. Without the human contact the child's mind easily wanders. Perhaps the only justification for using a tape is when travelling in a car; but is it really necessary to entertain children all the time? If one must, then what about guessing games involving the countryside through which you are travelling?

And then there is the television. Again the child is watching alone with no physical contact. The programme, however good, is presented by strangers and often accompanied by short fragmented pictures. The characters very often have limited, stereotyped and jerky gestures, which I have often observed in children who watch a lot of television. Above all, the child is passive — an unnatural state for a child to be in and stunting to the imagination.

It's rather like this: have you ever seen a film, say, *Rebecca* by Daphne du Maurier, and later read the book? As you read the book you simply cannot put the film-star characters out of your mind. Your imagination has been blunted. The reverse is true when you read the book first: your imagination has created all the characters and situations, and if you now see the film you may well be a little disappointed. The images from your imagination are extremely powerful. This shows in a small way what happens when a child watches television. All the images are there, already created for the child, and nothing is left to the imagination. If you must watch television, it would be better to watch together with Mum or Dad, so that you can talk about the programme later.

Getting started

Many people say that they cannot tell stories. Not so. Everyone can! It just takes a little practice. This book is here to help you. There are stories for children aged from three to seven years, grouped according to approximate age range. Of course there will be some variation as not all children develop at the same speed, so it's up to the teller to make the final choice.

No one will be bored and they will go to sleep satisfied and comforted. They will look forward to this "bedtime special". If you have children of mixed ages, start with a story suitable for the youngest and add another (or two!) for the older ones.

First, start with a short story and commit it to memory. Keep repeating it while you are doing those mindless tasks like washing-up and hoovering. Remember, the younger your audience, the more often they will want to hear that same story again and again. This will give you confidence.

The majority of the stories in this book have repetitive and recurring themes and phrases, especially those in the first section. For example *The Little Jug* (see page 21) goes to the village to find something for his friend the little girl to eat. He hops down the mountain — *HOP, HOP, HOP, HOP* — and goes to the baker, he hops home, he hops back to the village — *HOP, HOP, HOP, HOP* — then goes to the butcher etc. Once you have learned the basics of these simple stories, the repetition makes them easy to remember — for you and your children. They will keep you right if you don't stay with exactly the same scenario or even the same words as before: "You didn't say that last time!" Then you can go on to more complicated stories. You can also tell the story in instalments, so they go to sleep wondering what's going to happen next. But you must be firm. No giving way to "Please, Mum, just a bit more."

I often introduce a story by speaking directly to the children, and perhaps asking them some questions, to engage and involve them from the very start. For example, in *The Harp with Five Strings* (see page 129) I start by talking about musical instruments. After naming some instruments, I ask, "Can you tell me any others?" In *Giant Grummer's Christmas*, I ask the children to name types of cheese (see page 52). This is all part of making the experience active for young listeners and getting their imaginations working. You can interrupt the story at any point to involve children, by asking their opinions, asking them to guess what happens next or to explain ideas that they might not understand. You can use actions to emphasise parts of the story and add an extra dimension (see *Giant Grummer's Christmas*, page 52; *Ameliaranne and* the Green Umbrella, page 56–57; *How the Elephant Got its Trunk*, page 89). And as you become more experienced, you can get more creative — there are endless possibilities.

Creating a Mood

I started telling stories when I was very young to children who were still younger than I. As far as I can recall, they were not read from books but were told and they were entirely made up; they usually concerned flowers, fairies, gnomes and angels. This storytelling was not done regularly but sprang out of circumstances.

Later, when I had my own children, storytelling became more regular, especially at bedtime. In fact, bedtime was never a time of stress; it was always a time to be looked forward to. We established a ritual: bath, pyjamas on, meal, teeth brushed, curtains closed, candle lit and then a story or stories.

Children are fascinated by stories from "When I was a little girl (boy) ..." so that can be a good way to start. With older children one could first talk about what happened during the day, possibly sorting out some difficulty and looking forward to what's coming the next day. A night prayer is best said as the very last thing, before the tucking in and a good-night kiss.

After the experience of our own children, when I became a class teacher I simply could not imagine a lesson without a story. Of course, in the Steiner curriculum, all the stories are related to the subject being taught and are suited to the age group. After fifteen years as a class teacher in a Steiner-Waldorf school, I retired and started three kindergartens in succession in different parts of the country. In kindergarten, the story is the most important part of the day. The same story may easily be told for three weeks, so that it becomes fully integrated into the child's soul. I have never had a child complain about the repetition. During the three weeks we would also teach the parents puppetry and have them present a puppet show of (yes, again!) the same story, presented by the parents and told by the teacher. The children would go home fully satisfied and fulfilled, and were always given the opportunity to play peacefully and quietly so that the effect of the story was fully achieved.

Now, these are ideal circumstances where you are fully in charge. But I learned a great deal from my own experiences of telling stories in new environments with children I had not met before, such as playgroups. This was often a totally different experience: with music playing in the background, plastic toys strewn about, no established routine for a clear beginning or ending to a meal, hard metal or plastic chairs with no soft cushions and bright, aggressive colours on the walls. But ultimately none of this mattered. A small personal prayer to the angels did wonders! And I found that most helpers were only too willing to help create the mood I was striving for.

And then it was up to me to make the magic. I began by telling them my name and asking some of the children's names. I often told them about the olden days when grannies and grandpas lived with the family, and asked the children if they had grandparents who told stories about when they were children. All this breaks the ice.

In the meantime the children were seated on cushions on the floor or on small chairs. Then I would "magic" an ordinary chair into a storytelling chair by first covering it with a soft cloth so that it looked cosy. Then I transformed myself into a granny by putting a beautiful shawl over my shoulders. And then, out came the basket. It sat on a small fold-up table, covered with a coloured veil. I asked the children what colour it was, involving them all the time. I would always use a colour that was suitable for the season, for example, blue for Christmas, yellow for spring, red or orange for summer and violet or purple for autumn.

Next out of the basket came a candle-holder, a candle and matches. They were placed on the table and the candle was lit. Next came a lovely sounding bell, which was also laid on the table. And last, but not at all least, another little box. I asked the children, "Whatever can this be?" None of their suggestions were ever correct, because inside the box lived a little pin. I shook the box so that they could hear it. It was a very special pin: "When everyone is ready to listen, I will drop the pin, and when everyone is so still that we can hear the pin drop, then we are ready to begin." And then the bell was rung gently and purposefully. "ARE YOU READY?! Then I will begin ..."

I have seldom experienced a child disturbing the story. Should it be so, you can always appeal to the magical word MAY, as in "You may sit beside me" or "You may sit on my lap." This MAY does not mean MUST nor does it mean YOU ARE ALLOWED; it's a magical invitation that never fails. The child concerned will come forward as though in a trance and will do whatever you say. But, as I've said, there is seldom a need for it.

One occasion stands out clearly in my memory. It occurred in a playgroup that I visited regularly. The storytelling was kept to the end of the session, and mums and dads were already arriving to collect their offspring. The waiting room was separated from the storytelling area by a folding door. The mums and dads could not understand why it was so quiet in contrast to the usual rumpus at the end when helpers were tidying up and there was no particular routine; the children were just left to run about and let off steam. When the playgroup leader allowed the parents to peep though the folding door, they were amazed to see all the children sitting quite still and listening. I hope and pray that it left a lasting impression on the parents of what is quite easily possible.

Angels and fairies

Angels in a story bring the child into another realm of images. The more stories of this kind that you tell the child, the more the child is absorbed in a mood of awe and magic. Angels are often regarded as childish fiction. But, for small children, they are a reality. Even those who have never been told about angels — as I often experienced in various kindergarten groups — are immediately open to their being. It gives the child a safe and protected feeling to talk about angels almost daily. If you, yourself, can relate to such ideas, you can tell the children about their own Guardian Angel, who cares for and guides each person. You cannot see angels but you can sense them. You could tell them of angels who have different tasks, such as those who look after plants and those who look after animals. You can incorporate poems in the kindergarten or home routine by saying this well-known verse when the dolls are put to sleep.

> Matthew, Mark, Luke and John
> Bless the bed that I lie on.
> Four corners to my bed,
> Four angels there are spread.
> One at my head and one at my feet
> And two to guard me as I sleep.

It's a good idea to have a picture of an angel in the kindergarten and home, perhaps any of the beautiful Annunciation paintings by artists of the Renaissance, or a book with pictures of different angels, for instance, *Tobias and the Angel*.

Fairies can be a more approachable subject than angels for many parents. All children and grown-ups know about fairies; some lucky ones can even see them! The well-known series of books *Flower Fairies* by Cicely Mary Barker are widely available. Each painting is accompanied by a poem. Be sure to get the genuine article; there are some poor imitations.

Fairies are a reality for small children. Where possible we should encourage this, for dismissing other-worldly realities can inflict hurt on a small child who has a more universal awareness than the more down-to-earth adult. Here is a poem in which childish wonder and imagination is contrasted with matter-of-factness and even cynicism:

> One day when we went walking
> I found a dragon's tooth,
> A dreadful dragon's tooth.
> "A locust thorn," said Ruth.

> One day when we went walking
> I found a brownie shoe,
> A brownie's button shoe.
> "A dried peapod," said Sue.

> One day when we went walking
> I found a mermaid's fan,
> A merry mermaid's fan.
> "A scallop shell," said Dan.

One day when we went walking
I found a fairy's dress,
A fairy's flannel dress.
"A mullein leaf," said Bess.

Next time that I go walking
Unless I meet an elf,
A funny, friendly elf.
I'm going by myself.

— Valine Hobbs

Young children rarely ask at the end of a fairy story, "Is it really true?" But if they do ask, the answer must be, "Yes, of course it's true." You can say this, because the answer is required by the consciousness of the small child. And also because fairy tales do indeed contain truths about human life embodied in wonderful imagery and metaphors. The small child is at one with the world of magic and nature, and this includes fairies, elves, gnomes, wizards and angels.

As the child moves into further stages of development, fairies make way for other images. However, the fact that the child has lived with fairies at the appropriate stage of its development means that that stage has been fully realized and satisfied, and the child is ready to move on in an emotionally healthy way. There is no question of disillusionment. So to say to a small child that fairies are true is not lying to them; they are true at that stage in the child's development. In your stories, therefore, if you enter fully and imaginatively into the fairy realm, you will at the same time enter the stage of consciousness of the children in your care, whether at home, in the kindergarten or in the early years of school.

Animal stories

When we tell stories about animals we engender a feeling for animals, not only for those we have in our homes but also for animals in general.

Aesop's fables in which, more often than not, arrogance is humbled, are good examples, e.g. *The Grasshopper and the Ants, The Hare and the Tortoise, The Stork and the Fox.* Or they may be about the cleverness of animals, for example, *How the Fox rid himself of Fleas.* These fables are often a little sparse in the telling and the moral is presented as though to an adult; but they provide a wonderful basis for the imaginative storyteller to expand them in a way that suits small children. Here, for example, is the story of *The Lion and the Mouse* as told by Aesop:

> A Lion was awakened from sleep by a Mouse running over his face. Rising up in anger, he caught him and was about to kill him, when the Mouse piteously entreated, saying, "If you would only spare my life I would be sure to repay your kindness." The lion laughed and let him go.
>
> It happened shortly after this that the Lion was caught by some hunters who bound him by strong ropes to the ground. The Mouse, recognising his roar, came up and gnawed the rope with his teeth, and setting him free, exclaimed, "You ridiculed the idea of my ever being able to help you, not expecting to receive from me any payment of your favour; but now you know that it is possible for even a Mouse to confer benefits on a Lion.

Now, on page 71, I have retold this story of *The Lion and the Mouse* in a way that suits younger children. By imagining yourself as those characters and thinking how they would act in the situation, you can expand the story, choosing language that young children will understand. Think about the personalities of each character. The big, dominant lion has a high opinion of himself, so perhaps he talks in a deep voice, in an aloof and serious tone; the little mouse is cunning but meek, so perhaps he talks in an eager, high-pitched voice. Remember to involve your listeners and make the story an active experience for them. For example, when the lion falls in the pit and roars in anguish, I ask the question, "Who hears the roar?" The first time you tell the story, this will get the children thinking, and on subsequent tellings they'll be eager to get to this point where they know the answer and can join in.

The *Just So Stories* by Rudyard Kipling are a delight. Some are a bit too adult for young children but they are also easily adapted. Of course, all of these stories imbue the animals with human attributes, thoughts and emotions. But if the aim is to get a message across or to entertain, then it is entirely justified; and it's in tune with the small child's view of the world. You will find my retellings of some of Kipling's wonderful stories in the section for six to seven year-olds (*How the Zebra got its Stripes*, page 87; *How the Elephant got its Trunk*, page 89; *The Cat Who Walked Alone*, page 94).

Stories for special purposes

Some stories are created with a special purpose in mind. When a child is learning letters, it's wonderful to present a story first and then draw the letter. For example, for *Long-nose the Dwarf*, the letter could be L, N or D. Doing this brings life to what is otherwise an abstract mark. Let the child copy as large as possible and preferably in colour. These stories are all character forming; the perseverance of Long-nose is a wonderful example for small children. No lecturing is needed. The characters in these stories are all good role models. *Long-legs* and *The Mitten* are other suitable stories.

Using stories for learning numbers is another helpline. For this purpose in this collection I've included: *A Tale of Two Children, The Five Goats, A Tale of Nine Children, The Story of Ten Fingers* and *The Twelve Months*.

The story *The Star Child* has a special purpose too. In Steiner-Waldorf schools children create their own books, which they fill with pictures, letters of the alphabet and later stories that they write down from what they have heard and retell the next day. There are no lines on these pages and the child puts a star at each end of an imaginary line:

★   ★

The children then write the story between the stars. This gives an early feeling for spacing things on the page. Later they will learn to make more complicated stars, like the Star of David.

I hope that this book will start you off on the great adventure of telling stories to young children.

Beatrys Lockie

Stories for Children
Aged Three to Four

The Little Jug

Once upon a time there was a little girl who lived all by herself on top of a high hill. Well, not quite alone, because her best friend was a Little Jug. You all know what a jug is: sometimes it holds milk or flowers or just water.

One day the little girl opened her cupboard and it was completely empty — there was nothing to eat or drink! So she said to her friend, "Now, Little Jug, you need to go down to the village to find us something to eat."

But first she washed it in warm soapy water, then she rinsed it in cool spring water, then she dried it, and lastly she rubbed it with a special cloth until it was all shiny. Then she said, "Off you go now, my little friend, and bring us back something nice."

So the jug hopped down the mountain — *HOP, HOP, HOP, HOP* — until it came to the village. There it went to the baker's shop, where the baker, in his white hat and apron, was just setting out his goods in the window: white and brown bread, of course, and rolls and buns and all kinds of biscuits. And in the middle of it all was a beautiful birthday cake with four candles on it.

Well, the baker was so busy arranging it all very beautifully that he did not notice that, every now and again, something fell off the window sill; and who was standing under it? Yes, the Little Jug! And it caught all the things the baker dropped until it was full to the brim. Then it quickly slipped out of the shop and started to climb up the hill — *HOP, HOP, HOP, HOP* — until it came to the little girl's house and knocked on the door.

The little girl said, "Who's there?"

The jug answered, "Jug full!"

And when the girl opened the door and found her friend standing there, full to the brim with all sorts of goodies, she said, "Oh, you darling Little Jug, come in, and thank you."

They had a great time eating together but, all too soon, the food was finished. So the little girl said again, "Now, my friend, you must go back again to the village and find more food for us."

But first she washed it in warm soapy water, then she rinsed it in cool spring water, then she dried it, and lastly she rubbed it with a special cloth until it was all shiny. Then she said, "Off you go now, my little friend, and bring us back something nice."

So the jug hopped down the mountain again — *HOP, HOP, HOP, HOP* — until it came to the village.

Did it go to the baker's shop this time? No, it had already been there. This time it went to the butcher's shop, where the butcher, in his straw hat and striped apron, was just setting out all his goods in the window: pies and bacon, bones for soup, whole strings of sausages and much, much more. Well, he was so busy arranging it all very beautifully that he didn't notice that, every now and again, something fell off the window sill; and who was standing there? Yes, the Little Jug! And it caught all the things the butcher dropped until it was full to the brim. Then it quickly slipped out of the shop and started to climb up the hill.

But, you know, meat it much heavier than bread and the Little Jug had to stop and sit down to rest every now and then — *HOP, HOP ... rest ... HOP ... sit down ... HOP, HOP ... rest* — and at last it came to the little girl's house and knocked on the door.

The little girl said, "Who's there?"

The jug answered, "Jug full!"

And when the girl opened the door and saw her friend standing there full to the brim with all kinds of good things to eat, she said, "Oh, you darling Little Jug, come in, and thank you."

They had a great time eating together. The meat lasted more than a few days and the girl made soup with the bones. But in the end it was all finished. So the little girl said again, "Now, Little Jug, you need to go down to the village again to find us something to eat.

But first she washed it in warm soapy water, then she rinsed it in cool spring water, then she dried it, and lastly she rubbed it with a special cloth until it was all shiny. Then she said, "Off you go now, my little friend, and bring us back something nice."

So the Little Jug hopped down the mountain — *HOP, HOP, HOP,*

HOP — until it came to the village. Did it go to the baker's shop? No! Did it go to the Butcher's shop? No! Where could it go?

It went to the Town Hall. This was a very big building and inside sat many very clever men, who were counting pennies: "One, two, three ... twenty ... fifty ... seventy ... one hundred ... one thousand," and so on. And every now and again some of these pennies rolled off the table; and who was standing under the table catching all these pennies? Yes, the Little Jug, of course! Soon it was full to the brim and had to go home.

But, oh dear, it's load was now much heavier than things made of flour and even heavier than meat. So the Little Jug had to stop and rest many more times; it even fell asleep sometimes — *HOP, HOP ... rest ... HOP ... yawn ... HOP ... sleep ... HOP, HOP ... rest* — and at last it came to the little girl's house and knocked on the door.

The little girl said, "Who's there?"

The jug answered, "Jug full!"

But then a very strange thing happened: as soon as the little girl saw all that money she became very greedy indeed, and she forgot to thank the Little Jug for all its work! She poured the pennies on to the table and said, "Quick, quick, go back and get more money." She didn't thank the Little Jug, she didn't wash it in warm soapy water, she didn't rinse it in cool spring water, she didn't dry it and she didn't rub it with the special cloth until it was all shiny. She was thinking only of all the money she could get.

She put the jug straight back outside, and the Little Jug felt so sad at the way it had been treated that it did not look where it was going and tripped over a stone. It was only a tiny stone, but it was enough, and the poor, sad jug fell down and broke into a thousand pieces.

When the little girl saw what had happened, she realized how greedily she had behaved and how unkind she had been to her friend. She picked up all the pieces and glued them together again. She looked after the Little Jug until it was quite better and felt strong once more and could *HOP, HOP, HOP, HOP* again. After that, they had enough pennies to buy food, and they lived happily together.

The Mitten

Once upon a time, in the middle of winter, an old man walked through the forest and his dog followed behind him. As the two were walking along, one of his mittens fell in the snow.

Nibbler, the mouse, came along twirling his whiskers and looking at the world. He saw the mitten and thought it was as good as a palace. He stood in front of it and called out, " Who lives in this mitten?" No one answered for there was no one in sight. " I will live here by myself, " said Nibbler the mouse, and in he went and set up home.

Then Croaker, the frog, came along, with a jump, three long strides and a jump again. He called out, "Who lives in this mitten?"

"I do, Nibbler the mouse, and who are you?"

"I am Croaker the frog. Can I come in?"

"Yes, do, and make yourself at home." So the frog went in and the two of them began to live together.

Then a hare came running by, and called out, "Who lives in this mitten?"

"I do, Nibbler the mouse."

"I do, Croaker the frog. And who are you?"

"I am Bandylegs the hare, the hill-jumper. Can I come in?"

"Yes, do, and make yourself at home." So the hare put his ears down and went in. And the three of them began to live together.

Then a fox came running by, and called out, " Who lives in this mitten?"

"I do, Nibbler the mouse."

"I do, Croaker the frog."

"I do, Bandylegs the hare, the hill-jumper. And who are you?"

"I am Reynard the fox, the fine-talker. Can I come in?"

"Yes, do, and make yourself at home." So the fox went in and the four of them began to live together.

Then a wolf came prowling by, and called out, "Who lives in this mitten?"

"I do, Nibbler the mouse."

"I do, Croaker the frog."

"I do, Bandylegs the hare, the hill-jumper."

"I do, Reynard the fox, the fine-talker. And who are you?"

"I am Prowler the wolf, who lurks behind bushes. Can I come in?"

"Yes, do, and make yourself at home," said all four together. And the wolf went in and the five of them began to live together.

Then, from the middle of the forest, a wild boar came walking by. He called out, "Who lives in this mitten?"

"I do, Nibbler the mouse."

"I do, Croaker the frog."

"I do, Bandylegs the hare, the hill-jumper."

"I do, Reynard the fox, the fine-talker."

"I do, Prowler the wolf, who lurks behind bushes. And who are you?"

"I am Flat Nose the boar. Can I come in?"

"You are too fat. You probably won't fit in," said all five together.

"Well, I will try." And the boar squeezed in and the six of them began to live together.

And then a bear came along. He was very slow and heavy. "Who lives in this mitten?"

"I do, Nibbler the mouse."

"I do, Croaker the frog."

"I do, Bandylegs the hare, the hill-jumper."

"I do, Reynard the fox, the fine-talker."

"I do, Prowler the wolf, who lurks behind bushes."

"I do, Flat Nose the boar. And who are you?"

"I am Big-foot the bear. Let me in."

"We cannot let you in. There is no room," said all six together.

"Sit a little closer together then," said Big-foot the bear.

"All right then, if you make yourself a little smaller." Yes, the bear could just fit inside, and the seven of them began to live together inside the mitten.

In the meantime, the old man had noticed that he had lost his mitten. He turned round and began to search for it. The dog went in front and sniffed all the way. Suddenly, he saw the mitten. It was lying in the snow and was moving as if it were alive.

The dog began to bark: *Woof, woof, woof!*

The seven animals in the mitten got such a fright that they quickly jumped out and ran off into the forest

Then the old man came and picked up his mitten.

The Pearl-grey Cockerel

Once there was a cockerel who travelled round the world. On his way he found a letter. He picked it up with his beak and read:

> Pearl-grey cockerel, Pearl-grey hen,
> Countess goose, Abbess duck, Birdie goldfinch,
> We are going to Spring Chick's wedding.

The cockerel went on, and after a few steps he met the hen, who asked, "Where are you going, friend cockerel?"

"I am going to Spring Chick's wedding."

"Can I come along?"

"If you are mentioned in the letter, yes." He looked at it and read:

> Pearl-grey cockerel, Pearl-grey hen ...

"Yes, you are in it. Come along." And together they went.

After a little while, they met the goose. "Hello, dear hen and friend cockerel. Where are you going?"

"We are going to Spring Chick's wedding."

"Can I come along?"

"If you are mentioned in the letter, yes." And the cockerel unfolded the letter again and read:

> Pearl-grey cockerel, Pearl-grey hen,
> Countess goose ...

"Yes, you are in the letter. Let us go then." And off they walked.

Soon they met the duck. "Where are you going, dear hen, goose and cockerel?"

"We are going to Spring Chick's wedding."

"Can I come along?"

"Yes, if you are in the letter." The cockerel read:

> Pearl-grey cockerel, Pearl-grey hen,
> Countess goose, Abbess duck …

"Yes, you are in it, come along!"

Some way farther they met Birdie goldfinch. "Where are you going dear friends duck, goose, hen and friend cockerel?"

"We are going to Spring Chick's wedding."

"May I come along?"

"Sure, if you are in the letter." He opened the letter again and read:

> Pearl-grey cockerel, Pearl-grey hen,
> Countess goose, Abbess duck, Birdie goldfinch …

"Hey, you are in the letter, too!" And the five of them went on.

Then they met the wolf, who also asked where they were going.

"We are going to Spring Chick's wedding," answered the cockerel.

"Then I'm coming as well."

"Yes, if you are mentioned in the letter." The cockerel read through the letter, but the wolf's name was not in it.

"But I still want to go," said the wolf.

And because they were afraid of the wolf, the others answered, "Let's go then."

When they were a few steps farther, the wolf said, "I'm hungry."

The cockerel answered, "I don't have anything for you."

"Then I will eat you." And the wolf opened his mouth and swallowed the cockerel, feathers and all.

A little farther on, the wolf said again, "I'm hungry."

The hen gave him the same answer as the cockerel, and the wolf ate her up as well. And so he did with the goose and the duck.

The wolf and the goldfinch were the only ones left, and the wolf said, "Dear bird, I am still hungry."

"I don't want you to eat me. Catch me if you can!" said Birdie goldfinch.

The wolf opened his mouth and the bird flew on top of his head. The wolf did all he could to get hold of the bird, but Birdie goldfinch fluttered from here to there, hopped into a tree, on to a branch and back again on to the wolf's head or his tail; and this made the wolf furious.

When the wolf had tired himself out, Birdie goldfinch saw a woman coming towards them. She was taking food to the mowers in the meadow. The bird called to the wolf, "If you let me live, I'll see to it that you get a good meal of spaghetti and meat, which the woman is taking to the mowers in the meadow. If she sees me, she will want to catch me and I will fly and jump from one branch to another. She will put the basket down, and while she's chasing me you can eat everything!"

And indeed, when the woman saw the beautiful bird she came and stretched out her hand to catch it. But, just then, the goldfinch flew up. The woman put the basket down and ran after the bird. Then the wolf went to the basket and had a feast!

When she saw what the wolf had done, the woman cried, "Help! Help!" And all the mowers came running. One had a sickle, another had a stick, and that was the end of the wolf.

Out of the wolf's stomach, alive and well, jumped Pearl-grey cockerel, Pearl-grey hen, Countess goose and Abbess duck. And together with Birdie goldfinch they all went to Spring Chick's wedding.

The Tomten

When you are asleep, do you sometimes have dreams? Good dreams or bad dreams? I have! And I'm going to tell you about one of my dreams. I remember it so clearly, as if it really happened.

In my dream I saw a farm. It had a lovely farmhouse, surrounded by fields and woods. It was winter and the ground was covered with snow, a deep layer of white, downy snow. It was already midnight and the farmer and his wife, who worked very hard all day, were sound asleep in their bed and so were their children — a boy and a girl, who lived there too, of course.

The snow had covered everything over and yet I saw a trail of something. What was it?

It was footsteps! Tiny footsteps! To whom could they possibly belong?

And then I saw it: there was a tiny little man, a *Tomten*, and he went into all the stables where the animals slept to see if they were all right.

First he went to the cow's byre and spoke to the cows in his Tomten language that cows can understand, "Summers come and summers go, winters come and winters go. Soon you will be going out again into the meadows with buttercups."

Then he gave the cows some more hay and they *moo-ed* softly so as to thank him.

Now he went to the horse's stable. There stood Dobbin, the brown horse. And the Tomten said in his Tomten language that horses can understand, "Summers come and summers go, winters come and winters go. Soon you will be going out into the field with daisies again."

And he gave the horse some more to eat and Dobbin hinnied softly so as to thank him.

Then he went to the henhouse and said in his Tomten language that hens can understand, "Summers come and summers go, winters come and winters go. Soon you will be going out into the yard again to scratch for worms. Please, dear hens, will you lay me an egg for my supper?"

And the hens *tock-tocked* and *cluck-clucked* as if to say, "Feel under my soft feathers; there you will find a warm, new-laid egg for your supper."

"Thank you", said the Tomten. "Thank you kindly," and then he gave them all some more grain.

Then the Tomten went outside to see Glen in the dog's kennel, and spoke to him in his Tomten language that dog's can understand, "Summers come and summers go, winters come and winters go. Soon you will be out on the hill herding the sheep again. Are you cold tonight with all this snow? I shall fetch you some more straw to keep you warm, and then I shall break the ice in your water bowl and get some fresh water for you."

"Good, thank you," barked Glen softly so as not to waken the sleeping children.

"Good night," they said to each other.

Then the Tomten went into the farmhouse and saw the farmer and his wife sound asleep. Next door the two little children were sound asleep too and dreaming deeply. "What a pity they don't understand my Tomten language or I could speak with them," thought the Tomten. He tiptoed out carefully so as not to waken them.

Then he went to the barn where he always slept in the straw. The black and white cat was waiting for him and purring.

"Yes," said the Tomten, "I shall give you some nice warm milk from the cows, and then I shall have my egg that the hens gave me. Then the two of us, you and I, shall curl up together and go to sleep." And that is what they did.

And the fresh snow covered over all the tiny footsteps, and nobody knew the Tomten had been there except the cows, Dobbin the horse, the hens, Glen the dog and the black and white cat. And me.

The Easter Hare

Once upon a time there was a father Easter hare and a mother Easter hare. They had seven hare children, and only one of them would become the next real Easter hare, but they did not know which one.

So mother Easter hare took a basket with seven different eggs, and father Easter hare called all the seven hare children together.

He said to the eldest, "Take an egg from the basket and hide it in the garden of a house where children live."

The eldest hare picked the golden egg. He ran through the forest, jumped over a stream, came out of the forest, ran across the meadow and ended up in the garden of a house where children lived. He tried to jump over the fence, but he ran so fast and jumped so high that he dropped the egg and it broke. So he was not the real Easter hare.

Now it was the second hare's turn. He chose the silver egg. He took it from the basket and ran with it through the forest, jumped over the stream, came out of the forest and ran across the meadow. A magpie called suddenly, "Are you going to give that egg to me? If you do, I'll give you fifty pence." And before he really knew what was happening, the magpie had taken the silver egg back to his nest. So he was also not the real Easter hare.

Now it was the turn of the third hare. He took the chocolate egg, ran through the forest with it, jumped over the stream, came out of the forest, and just then a squirrel came down from a tall pine tree. She looked at him in astonishment and asked, "That will probably taste lovely."

"I don't know because it's for the children," answered the young hare.

"Can I have just a little taste?" The squirrel licked the egg. And, because it tasted so lovely, the hare had a lick as well ... and together they finished the whole egg! And when the third hare came home, his mother pulled his whiskers, which were still covered in chocolate, and said, "You are also not the real Easter hare."

Now it was the fourth hare's turn. The fourth hare chose the speckled egg. He ran through the forest and came to the stream. As he walked over the tree trunk that lay across the stream, he stood still for a moment to admire his reflection in the water. At that moment the egg rolled, *SPLASH*, into the water. So the fourth hare was also not the real Easter hare.

Now it was the fifth hare's turn. He took the yellow egg from the basket. He ran through the forest with it but, before he came to the stream, he met a fox, who said, "Come for a minute to my den. Then my children can admire that beautiful yellow egg as well." The hare went with the fox. The little fox cubs started playing with the egg immediately, until it dropped on a stone and broke. The hare quickly ran home and dropped his ears. He was also not the real Easter hare.

Now it was the turn of the sixth hare. This hare chose the red egg and ran through the forest with it. On his way he met another hare. Carefully he put his egg down by the side of the road and started to fight with the other hare — *SMACK ... SLAP ... SMACK* — they beat each other on the ears with their paws. Finally the other hare ran away. Then the sixth hare went to pick up his egg, but it had been trodden on during their fight. He was also not the real Easter hare.

Now it was the turn of the seventh hare. He was the youngest and smallest. For him only the blue egg remained in the basket. He ran through the forest with it. On his way he met another hare, but he just let him pass and continued on his way. Then the fox came towards him, but our little hare took to his heels and went straight to the stream. With a few careful hops on the tree trunk he reached the other side. On the edge of the forest the squirrel appeared, but the hare continued on its way and came to the meadow. The magpie tried to shout something to him, but the hare just answered, "I'm in a hurry! I'm in a hurry!"

Finally he reached the garden of the house. The gate was closed. He took a run and jumped, not too hard and not too high — *HOP* — over the gate. The children had made a little nest of grass for the Easter egg, and there he laid the blue egg. Yes. He was the real Easter hare.

The Star Child

When it's winter and it's night-time, what do you see in the sky? Yes, the moon, sometimes, but not always. But always there are stars — hundreds, no thousands — there are so many of them. Some are small, like pinpricks, and others have a very bright light, don't they?

Well, today I am going to tell you a story about a little star, a little baby star, who did not yet have a very bright light. His father had a beautiful strong light, almost red, and when people on earth looked up to the sky they felt strong and full of courage. The mother also had a beautiful light but it was different, it was more mellow, and when people on earth saw that, they knew that all mothers love their children.

Well, the little star child did not yet have a very bright light. It just did not get any brighter. The other star children were rather unpleasant about it and they teased him, saying, "Ha-ha! You can't shine. We're much better than you".

This made the star child very sad. He went to his father and mother and cried, "The other star children are teasing me because I can't shine. Will I ever be as bright as them?"

"Nonsense," said father star, "of course you will."

But mother star said, "I have heard of a very wise lady, who lives across the sky. We'll travel to her, for she'll know what to do. Don't worry, you'll be all right."

Well, the next night they got ready for their long journey. Now, you and I are awake during the day when it is light and asleep during the night when it is dark. But for stars it is just the opposite, of course. They do their work at night; they shine in the dark, don't they?

So as soon as it got dark that night they set off across the sky. What a lot of stars they met, old and new, and at last they came to the Evening Star, where the wise old woman lived. They knocked at the gate and a sweet star lady opened it.

She said, "Ah! There you are! You are very welcome! Our lady is sitting beside her star pond, playing her lyre."

Soon they found her, and what a lovely wise face she had! She said, "I have heard all about you and your trouble. Come with me. I know just what to do." They followed her into her house, straight into the kitchen.

"Now," she said, "we're going to bake some star biscuits. Not ordinary star biscuits like we make at Christmas; no, special star biscuits with a magic powder in them." She set the star child to work, showing him patiently what to do, and when all the dough had been rolled out and cut into star shapes, she took a tin from a high shelf and said, "Open it. Go on." When the star child took the lid off he almost had to shut his eyes, such a glow came out of the box.

"Now sprinkle some of this magic dust over the biscuits you prepared and then we shall put them into the oven."

The star child did as he was told, and after a while a heavenly smell spread throughout the kitchen. After ten minutes they were ready and taken out of the oven. My goodness! How they shone!

"Have some, as many as you like," said the star lady.

Well, they did not need to be asked again. They were absolutely delicious, mouth-watering! But not only did they taste scrumptious, a very strange thing began to happen: the star child began to shine! First a little, then more, and then so strongly that they could not believe it.

Oh dear, the night was getting on and they had to get home before the sun rose. They thanked the kind star lady very much and then flew across the sky, past all their friends the stars, and got home just before it got light.

The next night, as soon as it got dark, the little star child was longing to show his new shine. When he got out into the darkness the other star children said, "Oh, look at that lovely shining star! It's the star child who could not shine. What has happened to him?"

The star child told them about his adventure and they never teased him again. And, what's more, they became good friends.

The Little Star's Search

Once upon a time there was a little girl who liked to look up at the stars in the sky. The more she looked up, the more she wished she could be among the stars and play with them. Yes! That is what she most wanted! During the day, when she could not see the stars, she was often sad.

Well, one day she stood by a pond and she said to the pond, "I want to play with the stars in the sky. Can you help me?"

The pond answered, "The stars? Oh, they shine upon me every night so brightly I can hardly sleep! Perhaps if you swim in me you can find the stars."

So the little girl went into the pond and swam around, but she did not find any stars. And the pond said, "I'm sorry I couldn't help you. Why not try the little stream that flows in the wood?"

The little girl went to the stream and said, "Please, dear stream, can you help me? I want to play with the stars."

The stream answered, "The stars? They glitter on my waves every night. Perhaps if you paddle in me you may find them."

So the little girl went into the stream and the water came up to her knees, but she could not find any stars. And the stream said, "I'm so sorry I couldn't help you. Perhaps the little folk, the gnomes, can help you. You will find them in the wood everywhere."

The little girl walked through the woods and soon she came upon a band of little gnomes and she said to them, "Dear gnomes, I would like so much to play with the stars. Can you help me?"

The gnomes said, "The stars? Oh, they shine every night on the grass here. Come, dance with us on the grass and perhaps you will find them."

So the little girl danced with the gnomes; round and round they danced, but she could not find any stars. And the gnomes said, "We're sorry we couldn't help you, but you can try something else: ask Four-Feet to carry you to No-Feet and then ask No-Feet to carry you to the Stairs-Without-Steps. If you climb the Stairs-Without-Steps you will surely find the stars."

The little girl went along and soon she met a horse. "Dear Four-Feet, will you carry me to No-Feet please?"

"Come along then, climb on my back and I will carry you to No-Feet."

The little girl climbed on to the horse's back and Four-Feet ran and ran with her until they came to the sea. Four-Feet said, "Well, here we are. Get down now and wait here for No- Feet. The little girl climbed down and waited while the horse galloped off back to the wood.

She did not have to wait long for soon a big fish came swimming along. The little girl said, "Please No-Feet, can you take me to the Stairs-Without-Steps?"

"All right," said the fish. "Get up on my back and I'll take you to the Stairs-Without-Steps." And the little girl did that, and the fish swam and swam until he was far out to sea. Then the little girl saw a wide glistening path on the sea, and at the end of that path there was something that looked like a staircase going up and up into the sky. But these stairs were made of all colours of the rainbow; they shimmered red and blue and pink and yellow.

"Well," said the fish, "here you are. Go on that glittering path until you come to the colourful stair that you see at the end of it."

And the little girl climbed down from the fish and walked on the glittering path of the waves until she came to the stairs; but they had no steps, only colours: red, blue, pink, green and yellow. So the little girl put her hands on the blue and her feet on the red and started to climb. She climbed and climbed from one colour to another. At long last, she came to the top of the stairs and there she saw many, many beautiful angels and each angel held a shining star.

The girl said, "Oh, dear angels, I have come a long way because I want so much to play with the stars."

And the angels answered, "But, dear, you come to us every night when you are asleep. Every night when you sleep you are with us and you play with the stars!"

When the girl heard this she was very happy, so happy that she closed her eyes, and when she opened them again she was in bed and the sun was shining in through the window. But she still felt happy, for she knew now that she was with the angels every night, playing with the stars.

Stories for Children
Aged Five to Six

A Farm Story

Once upon a time there was a farmer and his wife. They were very poor in that they had little money, and yet they were rich in that they were healthy and loved each other.

But the one great sadness and emptiness in their lives was that they had no children, and however hard they prayed to God to fulfil this wish, it seemed that he would not listen.

After the long hard winter, at last the beams of the sun began to feel a little warmer. The farmer and his wife felt grateful because soon the day would come when their sheep and cows would give birth to their young ones.

But, how sad! The first sheep lost her little lamb. The mother sheep kept calling for her lamb and the people on the farm felt sorry for her.

Now, when the second sheep's lamb was born, there was more unhappiness. This time the mother sheep died, leaving her newborn lamb all cold and lonely.

"Oh, dear husband," said the wife, "what shall we do? It is as if God wants to punish us for something."

"No, no, dear wife," answered the farmer, "never, ever think that. God is good and will not punish us; he only asks us to do our very best. Look, I know what to do."

And he took the skin of the dead lamb and put it on the poor bleating one. When the mother sheep smelled the skin of her dead lamb she thought it was her own and started to look after it. It was wonderful to see, and quite soon the little lamb drank warm sweet milk from its new mother and then laid itself against her and fell sound asleep.

The farmer and his wife looked after them both well, as they did with all their animals and their plants in the garden. When autumn came, the wife felt that at last she too would become a mother.

The next year a baby girl was born to them. Now there was even more work as they had the new baby to look after as well as all the farm animals. But, although the days were long and the work never seemed to end, the farmer and his wife never forgot to be grateful to God for granting their wish.

The girl grew up sweet and strong like her parents. Soon she began to help on the farm. Of course, she loved to feed the hens and she learned to milk the cows. But what she liked most was feeding the orphaned lambs with a bottle of milk. When her father and mother saw her doing that, they remembered how the mother sheep had taken to the little lamb with her dead baby's fleece on it.

And they lived happily ever after. They never became rich but God blessed them with a lovely family.

How the Snowdrop Got its Colour

After Father God had created all the plants and flowers, he wanted to give them beautiful colours. So he gave the forget-me-not blue, the marigold orange, the iris purple, the roses pink, red and yellow, and so on until they were all done. The angels were very busy painting the flowers all the colours of the rainbow and when they were ready they looked beautiful.

But what the angels forgot was that, while they were painting all the flowers of spring, summer and autumn, there was one little flower that had grown up, flowered and faded before any of the others had even appeared. It was the very first flower of the year; yes, it was the snowdrop.

When the snowdrop heard that all the other flowers had been given colours, while it was still green like grass and leaves, it was sad that it had been missed out. "Why me?" it sighed. "I know that I'm only little, but I too would like to have a colour. I know, I'll ask the other flowers to give me a little of theirs. They are sure to agree."

So up the snowdrop went to a yellow tulip. "Please, Mr Tulip, could you share some of your yellow with me as I haven't got any colour?"

"What?" said the tulip. "I need it all for myself. When I flower in spring there usually isn't much sun yet and I have to shine as hard as I can."

The snowdrop understood and thanked the tulip nicely.

Next it saw a forget-me-not. "Please, Miss Forget-me-not, can you give me some of your beautiful blue because they have left me out?"

The forget-me-not answered, "Blue, blue, not for you; blue's for me, for me, you see." And on and on it went, saying the same words over and over again.

The marigold was next. "Please, Mrs Marigold, may I have some of your cheerful orange; I only need a little. You see, they have forgotten me."

"Some of my beautiful bright sunny orange? It wouldn't suit you at all; it only suits me. Try another flower" And so saying she turned her back on the poor snowdrop.

They all seemed to be the same; they didn't want to share. Should the snowdrop just stop now and try to be content with no colour? No, it would have one more go.

It approached a lovely red rose with the same request. But the snowdrop had hardly finished speaking when the haughty rose gave the snowdrop a nasty prick with its thorns. "Never! It's all mine. It was given to me and it stays with me."

The snowdrop was not only sad; it was a little offended. Never was it going to ask for a favour again. In its sorrow it bent its head right down. And then it started to snow. When the snow saw the sad little plant, it whispered, "What's happening here and why are you so bent down?"

The snowdrop sighed and told the snow that all the plants had colours and that the angels had forgotten it. And so the snowdrop was left all green, like grass and leaves. How it longed for a colour of its very own.

"That's easy," said the snow, "I'll give you some of mine. I have plenty to share." So the snow started to cover the snowdrop with a white, pure and clean, until it looked beautiful.

But, you know, if you look carefully at the snowdrop flower, you will see a few bits of green that the snow did not quite cover up.

From that day onwards, the snowdrop and the snow were very good friends; that is why they always come together. "I will not harm you with my cold," promised the snow.

People love the snowdrop as it is the very first flower in spring, and it gives them hope after the dark days of winter.

Lassie

This is the story of a very lovely dog who was called Lassie. She really was the most obedient and the most faithful dog in the whole wide world. Her master was a woodcutter, and as he left for work early in the morning, he swung his axe over his shoulder and whistled his favourite tune.

"Cheerio, dear children. I shall see you again tonight," he said.

And to his wife, "Goodbye, dear wife. I shall bring you home another load of fine wood to keep us all warm and for you to cook our supper on."

Well, off he went and soon he came to the spot where he had stopped the day before. The wood he had cut lay in neat heaps all around and he chose a big tree and started work. He got on so well that he didn't notice the sun going down between the trees.

"Goodness me," he said, "how the time has flown! I had better go home soon or it will be dark. You know what, instead of going the long safe way, I'll take the shortcut across the boggy moor. That will be quicker." And so he did.

When he came to the marshy bit, he knew exactly what to do. Carefully he stepped on the tufts of the rushes so as not to fall into the bog. But, oh! He slipped and his foot got stuck in the bog.

"I shall throw off the bundle of logs," he thought, "then I will be lighter and it will be easier to get unstuck." But it did not work. The only thing left to do was to throw away his heavy axe, but then he would no longer be able to look after his family by keeping them warm. And then he thought of his dog; Lassie would know what to do! But would she hear him from inside the house?

"Lassie! Lassie!" he called, and again, "Help, Lassie!" *(Ask the children to join in.)*

By now it was almost dark and Lassie was lying by the fire waiting for her master to come home. Suddenly she pricked up her ears and then she got up, whining and scratching at the door, wanting someone to open it.

"That's strange," said the mother, "I didn't hear anything. But then, dogs have much better hearing than people."

So she opened the door, and as Lassie shot out in the direction of the bog, she heard it too: "Lassie, Lassie! Help me, help me! Please! I'm stuck on the moor!"

Quickly the mother got a ladder from the side of the shed and ran after the dog. Lassie had already reached the spot and barked to his master, as if to say, "Don't worry now, I'm here!" She knew just what to do. She stepped carefully on the tufts and when she reached her master, she started to dig a path. After some time she pulled her master very gently out.

In the meantime the mother had arrived and had put the ladder across so that the woodcutter could step on to the rungs. When at last he reached safety, his wife said, "Thank God that you are safe again."

"Yes," said the woodcutter, "I thank God that I am safe again, but I also thank him for giving us Lassie, for without her I would have disappeared into the bog."

So they hugged their most obedient and most faithful dog and praised her. She wagged her tail with pleasure and licked their hands. She had understood every word they said.

Hendrika's Adventure

There was once a farmer who had many cows, but there was one that he loved the most and she was called Hendrika. Now, Hendrika lived in a meadow among many meadows surrounded by ditches and canals. And across the canal there was the farmer's house and a windmill and a road.

In the next field there lived a horse called Peter and he was Hendrika's best friend. Peter told Hendrika about everything he saw when he was away with the farmer selling cheeses in town: about the many very high houses, churches and towers, cars, people on bicycles, shops with lots of different things in them, and boats, and lots and lots of people.

All day Hendrika ate grass and buttercups and daisies, and she got fatter and fatter. Hendrika's master, the farmer, was very pleased with her as she gave him so much lovely milk from which he made butter and cheese and yoghurt. So he always said to her, "Eat, Hendrika, eat and make more milk."

But Hendrika got bored with doing the same thing every day: eating and eating and eating. How Hendrika wished she could see all the exciting things that Peter the horse told her about. But no, all she could do was eat, eat, eat.

Then one day she saw some delicious buttercups growing at the side of the canal. She tried to taste them but, as she was so fat, she fell over and found herself in the river! It so happened that an empty raft floated within her reach.

"This is my chance," thought Hendrika. "It will take me to the place that Peter has told me all about."

With some difficulty she clambered on to the raft and started to float away. How delightful! Past the farmer's house, past the windmill, past all the other cows standing in their boring fields eating the boring grass, and finally into the city!

People were gathering all around. Never had they seen a cow floating on a raft! At one point two boys pulled her ashore, and for the first time Hendrika felt hard cobblestones under her hooves instead of soft ground.

It was just as Peter had described: many, many houses and some so very high, towers, churches with spires, shops with all sorts of things in them, bicycles, boats and lots and lots of people. She did enjoy it all! At last, she found herself in a big square where people were dressed in special clothes selling cheeses; and who did she see there? Yes, it was Mr Dykstra, the farmer, her master. His mouth fell open with surprise.

"Hendrika, what are you doing here instead of eating grass in the meadow?"

She didn't even hear him, because her attention was caught by a stall where they were selling straw hats decorated with flowers. She quickly snatched one and put it on her horns. Never did a cow look so pretty.

But soon she was caught, and put into a cart that Peter, her friend, pulled and brought home again. How nice and soft the field felt to her feet that were tired with walking on the hard cobblestones.

Although it had been a great adventure, Hendrika was really glad to be back. Now that she had seen all these things for herself, she could talk about it with her friend Peter. And, actually, she was very hungry now. She ate as much grass and as many daisies and buttercups as she could, and she didn't find them at all boring!

Miaula and the Twins

Once there was a family who had a cat. Her name was Miaula. She was big and fat and black all over, except for her white bib and the very tip of her tail. There were three children in that family: Peter the eldest, and the twin boys whose names were Binky and Dinky. Miaula really belonged to the twins.

You can imagine how much they loved her, so, when she disappeared one day, they were very, very sad and no one could comfort them.

First, mother tried: "I shall buy you a new pussycat." But, oh no, they didn't want a new pussycat; they wanted Miaula back. And they cried themselves to sleep at night with big tears clinging to their chubby cheeks.

Father tried another way: "If you don't stop that infernal noise, I shall smack you with my leather slipper." That stopped the twins for a moment, but not for long.

Then Peter had an idea: "C'mon, boys," he said. "We're going to look everywhere all over again, inside and outside."

They started in the garden. They looked under bushes, in rabbit holes, ditches, up trees, and unlocked the doors of the greenhouse and the garden shed. Now for inside. They opened drawers, looked on shelves and under the beds. They searched the attic and the cellar. No sign of Miaula.

Binky and Dinky, the twins, would not eat and were getting thin and pale.

That night, when the twins had finally fallen asleep, Peter was still wide awake. Had they perhaps forgotten some place? He could not get to sleep for worrying about it.

The bedroom door was standing ajar with a faint light shining in from the passage. Suddenly it was pushed open a little wider and, who do you think came in? It was Miaula! And she was carrying something in her mouth. Peter couldn't see what it was.

In one jump she leaped on to the twins' bed. She made a little hollow and placed a tiny kitten in it. She licked it for a moment and jumped off the bed again. After a few minutes she was back with another fluffy kitten and did the same thing all over again. Twice more she did the same. So how many little kittens were there now on the bed?

Peter was so fascinated that he simply could not move, but once Miaula had licked all her babies and settled down, he slid out of bed and woke the twins.

They shouted with joy! "Oh look! Miaula has come back to us and she has brought four darling kittens." The twins made such a noise that their nanny, who slept next door and who was there to help Mum look after them, awoke with a start and rushed through to see what was going on.

Now Nanny did not like cats. She had often said that they were dirty beasts, and she was glad that Miaula had got herself lost. One thing you can certainly say about cats is that they are not at all dirty, for they are forever washing themselves. But when Nanny came into the room and saw not only Miaula but also four extra little cats — and on top of the bed — she lost her patience and smacked first Binky then Dinky.

Well now, they had not done anything wrong and they started to cry, and so Mum woke up. And soon after that, Dad too. Mum tried to calm the situation and said to Dad, "Go up to the attic and fetch my old sewing basket; it should be just big enough to fit them all." Once the four kittens were put in the basket, Miaula soon followed, and at last everyone could get back to sleep.

But if you think that's the end of the story, you are quite mistaken. Just when Peter was dropping into a deep sleep, Miaula jumped on to his bed and patted his left cheek.

Half awake, Peter said, "Yes, Miaula, your babies are beautiful. Go back to them now and let me sleep." But she would not go! This time she patted his right cheek and mewed loudly.

"Oh, Miaula," Peter said, "don't do this, I want to go to sleep!" But this time Miaula almost scratched him and called all the more, so that Peter woke up altogether.

As he sat up, he smelled something. It was smoke. Now, Peter knew that where there is smoke there is usually fire, so he jumped out of bed, woke up the twins, then ran along the passage knocking loudly on Nanny's and his parents' doors.

"Wake up, wake up, the house is on fire!" he shouted. They all put on their dressing gowns and slippers quickly and ran outside, mother carrying Miaula and the kittens in their basket while father telephoned the fire brigade.

The fire brigade arrived with lots of sirens going and bells ringing, and the firemen soon unrolled their hoses, put up their ladders and started to hose water on to the flames. In no time at all they had the blaze under control.

The house was full of smoke so they couldn't possibly sleep inside, so mother suggested that they roll up in blankets and sleep all together in the summerhouse. "Just like soldiers", she said; Miaula in her basket as well, of course. It was great fun!

Next morning, father went to see the silversmith in town. Do you know what a silversmith is? He is not the kind of smith who puts shoes on horses; a silversmith makes fine bracelets and rings, not of steel but of silver.

"Can you do a job for me?" father asked.

"Of course," answered the silversmith, "that's what I'm here for." Then father told him the whole story of Miaula.

"I would like to make a small silver medal with the following inscription: I AM MIAULA, WHO WARNED PETER WHEN THE HOUSE WENT ON FIRE. Can you do that for me?"

"Of course," said the smith. "It will be ready tomorrow."

Next day, father went back and was pleased with what the smith had made. He thanked him and paid him and went home to show it to the family.

Mother said, "I have the very thing to hang it round her neck with," and from her sewing basket she drew a red velvet ribbon and threaded it through the little hole in the silver medal. They fastened it around Miaula's neck. How proud and grand Miaula looked as she walked around the house. Even Nanny was grateful to her!

Sometimes visitors wonder what is written on the medal. They are always amazed when they read it: I AM MIAULA, WHO WARNED PETER WHEN THE HOUSE WENT ON FIRE.

Giant Grummer's Christmas

Giant Grummer was a very bad giant. He did not believe in Christmas so he never kept it. Sometimes on Christmas Day he would sit in his huge castle eating pickles and drinking vinegar all day long! Christmas was a very *sour* day for Giant Grummer. Just to think of so many people being so happy gave him a headache. Giant Grummer was a very bad giant!

He lived in a castle made of ... cheese! Now, there are lots of different kinds of cheese. Who can tell me the name of a cheese? Yes: Cheddar, Brie, Gouda, Edam. And there are some very bad-smelling cheeses like Esrom and Stilton. But the very worst of them all is *Limburger cheese*, and that's what the giant's castle was made from. No one in the village could or would come within a mile of the castle without being overcome (*demonstrate*). But Giant Grummer loved Limburger cheese. He loved it so much that he kept eating away at great chunks of his own castle: the towers and the walls even!

One Christmas Giant Grummer was even grumpier than before. He told the villagers that on Christmas Eve, after Santa Claus had been, he would reach his long arm down every chimney of every house and grab every stocking hanging at the fireplaces with presents in them! Then he would carry them over to his castle, spread them out on the floor and stamp on them until they were all broken into pieces. Just imagine! The poor children! The villagers were terribly worried when they heard this. But what could they do?

Now, there was not just one castle in the village, but two. Not two built of Limburger cheese. Oh no! The other was more like a palace and in it lived a little prince called Topsy-Turvy, and I'll tell you how he got that strange name.

He was only a little boy but he was not at all afraid of that big giant, however bad he was. Nor of his castle made out of Limburger cheese, for ... Topsy-Turvy had discovered that if he turned his nose upside down, everything smelled just the opposite of what it usually did: his mother smelled like cod liver oil, and Limburger cheese smelled like cookies and gingerbread.

When Prince Topsy-Turvy heard about Giant Grummer's plans, he went straight to the telephone and called Santa Claus. They had a long talk together and hatched a wonderful plan.

Giant Grummer had never hung up his stocking at Christmas, not even when he was a wee giant. His mother had told him that there was no such thing as Santa Claus. But the fact was that Santa Claus knew the smell of Limburger cheese would make his reindeer sick, deadly sick, so he never tried to get there.

Well, this Christmas, Giant Grummer received a very nice letter from Santa Claus. It said:

Dear Giant Grummer,

Why don't you hang up your stocking on Christmas Eve? I have some very nice presents that I would like to put in it. This would be much more fun than stealing the children's presents.

Your good friend,
Santa Claus

"Ho, Ho!" shouted Giant Grummer. "Ho, ho! I'll fool old Santa Claus. I'll hang my biggest stocking up and I'll watch him fill it. Then I'll dump the presents on the floor and I'll still have time to go over to the village and *snatch* all the children's presents." And he rubbed his hands and stamped his feet in glee (*audience participation*). Giant Gummer was a *very bad giant*.

So, on Christmas Eve, Giant Grummer came into the huge living room of his castle and hung up his great big stocking in front of the fireplace. It was *enormous*! Then he went off to bed and lay very still. He tried to stay awake and watch for Santa, but the first thing he knew, he was fast asleep, and he never clapped eyes on Santa at all!

At midnight Prince Topsy-Turvy met Santa in the village. "But how will we ever drive up to Limburger Castle?" asked Santa.

"I'll show you," said Topsy-Turvy. Then he turned Santa's nose upside down, and together they turned the noses of the eight reindeer! Topsy-Turvy jumped into the sleigh with Santa Claus and they started out for Giant Grummer's castle. Faster and faster they went. For now Limburger Castle smelled like cookies and gingerbread, and all eight reindeer were very fond of cookies and gingerbread!

On they went, right up on the roof of the castle. Down the chimney went Santa. When he saw the huge stocking he drew a long breath, but at once he began to fill it. First he put in a real motorcar. Then a big tin horn, and then pounds and pounds of sweets and cakes and gingerbread. Then, last of all, he pulled out of his sack lots of round cheeses. Can you imagine what kind of cheese? Yes! Limburger cheese! They were the very oldest and strongest-smelling Limburger cheeses. They were simply *awful*! Santa put these cheeses on top of the stocking, then he went up the chimney and drove away.

Soon it was morning. Before daylight Giant Grummer came running into the room to look at his stocking. As soon as he found the big foul-smelling cheeses, he didn't look for anything else. He just sat down on the floor and began to eat them. He ate up two whole cheeses. But when he tried to eat the third, he could not go on. He was just too full. His eyes began to close and soon he was fast asleep.

Giant Grummer slept all through Christmas morning and through Christmas afternoon and Christmas evening, and that is the reason why Giant Grummer was good all day. He was sound asleep.

Ameliaranne and the Green Umbrella

Ameliaranne and her five little brothers lived in a small cottage. Their mother took in washing from other people to earn enough money for them to live on. Their village was more or less like most villages, in that it had a church, a school, a store and an inn. But in one way it was very different: it had a manor house that belonged to a very special man. His name was Sir John and he was always very kind. One day each year, on his birthday, he invited all the children from the village to a big party. There was music and games and a never-to-be-forgotten huge tea with sandwiches, cakes, sweets fruits and, of course, an enormous birthday cake.

Sir John also had a sister who was called Lady Louise but she was not so nice, as you will hear in this story.

The day before the party, Ameliaranne's mother had put curlers in her daughter's hair because it was awfully straight and Ameliaranne had always dreamed of having ringlets. Her dress and her brothers' suits were washed, starched and ironed.

But, alas, on the day of the party, the little boys all had fearful colds: they were coughing and sneezing and they just had to stay in bed. They howled with disappointment. Ameliaranne wished she could do something to help them, but she could not think of anything. However, as she left for the party she saw her mother's green umbrella standing by the back door. Quickly she picked it up and carried on to the party at the manor house. From a distance she could see lights shining from all the windows and doors, and hear the strain of music.

Sir John stood at the entrance, splendid in his evening clothes. He knew all the children of the village by name. "Hello, Ameliaranne; how pretty you look. But where are all your brothers?" Ameliaranne told him the whole story and how the little boys were so sad not to be there.

Now, at the foot of the tall staircase stood Lady Louise, very stiff and upright, and watching carefully all that was going on. She took Ameliaranne's coat and was about to grab the umbrella when Ameliaranne said anxiously, "No, no, I need my umbrella."

Lady Louise retorted with a cold smile, "You can be sure it is not raining upstairs." And again she tried to pull the green umbrella from Ameliaranne. But Ameliaranne held on tight and managed to keep the umbrella, which she took upstairs with her.

The dancing was in full swing and the music set everyone's feet tapping (*demonstrate*). Ameliaranne stayed in her seat because she did not want to leave the umbrella. With the games it was the same: she stayed an onlooker.

Then came the highlight of the party: the *food*. Some children were greedy and took the best things first, and some stretched in front of others and helped themselves without being asked. Ameliaranne accepted all that was offered to her.

At last, all the plates were empty and it was time to go home. Ameliaranne was the last to leave.

Lady Louise jumped forward, saying, "I shall help you on with your coat, Ameliaranne, and now we shall see why you wanted that umbrella so much." She snatched the umbrella from the little girl and, oh dear, down fell cakes and sweets, sandwiches and fruit and one big piece of squashed birthday cake.

"Now we see, you greedy girl—"

But she couldn't finish her sentence, because Sir John interrupted her, saying, "Stop that at once, Louise. I have been watching Ameliaranne all evening and she hasn't eaten a single thing. She put it all in the umbrella and I bet it's for her little brothers who are ill in bed. Am I not right, Ameliaranne?"

Ameliaranne, a little shame-faced, nodded. Lady Louise slunk away, and Sir John clapped his hands and a servant appeared.

"William, take this girl to the kitchen and prepare a basket of food for the family, full to the brim." And with a wink to the butler, he whispered, "And don't forget the extras. Goodbye, Ameliaranne; I hope your brothers will be well again soon."

And so it happened that Ameliaranne came home with a heavy basket full of goodies. There was also a big bottle of lemonade and a large slice of birthday cake wrapped separately in kitchen paper. Ameliaranne put the basket on the bed in front of her brothers and mother took off the napkin. You should have seen their faces! There was enough delicious food for two days *(action: pat tummies and lick lips)*.

Ameliaranne put the umbrella back behind the door and softly whispered to it, "Thank you, umbrella. Tomorrow I shall clean you because you are all sticky."

The next day Ameliaranne's mother washed and ironed the napkin and Ameliaranne took the basket back; and she picked a big bunch of marigolds for Sir John.

Joanna and the Jumble Sale

School was over for the day. Most of the boys and girls had set off for home, but Joanna stood looking at the notice board in the passage. Pinned on it was a poster that has been beautifully painted by Joanna's teacher, Miss Helen Loveday. The poster said:

GRAND JUMBLE SALE
IN AID OF THE RED CROSS
TO BE HELD IN SLEEPY FURROW VILLAGE HALL
ON SATURDAY AFTERNOON.
PLEASE BRING CONTRIBUTIONS TO THE HALL
BY FRIDAY EVENING.

Joanna was just admiring all the little drawings in the border of the poster when Miss Loveday came out of the classroom.

"Would you like to help me at the jumble sale tomorrow, Joanna. We have lots of things already, and I'll be glad of help on my stall."

"Oh, Miss Helen, I would love to! But I'll have to ask mother first, because I usually help her with the little ones on Saturday."

With that Joanna lost no time in getting home. In fact, she ran all the way so that when she burst into the kitchen she only had enough breath left to gasp, "Oh, Mum! Miss Helen has asked me to help her on her stall tomorrow. I would love to help her but I said I helped you with the babies on Saturday."

"Why, bless the child," said Mother, quite taken aback. "You talk so fast I can't make head nor tail of it."

Mother sat down heavily in her favourite chair and Joanna said it all over again, much slower. When she had come to the end, Mother thought for a moment and then she said, "Well, Joanna, I don't see why you shouldn't go. We can soon do the house in the morning and then send William up to play with Farmer Wheatsheaf's children. He says that he's always pleased to have them and that means I could go to the sale myself."

Joanna's face beamed with pleasure as she sat down to her tea. She was just spreading honey on wee William's bread when Mother set her cup down and said, "I've been thinking, Joanna. After tea, you could take the things I've put together for the jumble sale up to the hall. They are sure to be busy up there and you can help Miss Loveday with the ticketing."

So directly after tea Joanna put on her hat and took the bundle of clothes that Mother had put together in one hand, and a box of scones for the food stall in the other, and set off up the road.

As soon as Joanna came to the village green she saw a crowd of boys and girls all making for the hall, each carrying a basket or a bundle. There were the Jollyface twins, struggling with one of their father's prize marrows, and Betty Button, whose mother was a dressmaker and who could make all sorts of pretty things out of bits and pieces. And then there was Teddy Carter, who had done his parcel up himself. He was proud of his slipknots, which he had learned at the Cub Scouts.

When Joanna stepped into the village hall, it seemed so full of people and of clothes that she hardly knew what to do, but Miss Loveday soon saw her.

"Here I am, Joanna," she called. "Come and help me sort the goods out."

Joanna first set down her bundle then she gave the scones to Miss Munday at the food stall. And then she knelt down beside Miss Loveday and began to sort out a big pile of clothes.

First she found all the loose socks, rolled them up in pairs as her mother did after wash day and put them on one side. Then she found a cushion, a scarf and a coloured ball, and placed them between a pile of books and an old straw hat. Then she came to a sailor suit that Tommy Tucker used to wear until he grew out of it. And last of all she found a pair of little blue slippers, which she gazed at for a long time. Joanna thought they were the prettiest slippers that she had ever seen! Each was made to look like a little rabbit with two fluffy white ears. There were beads for eyes, and the nose, the mouth and even the whiskers were worked in white silk.

"Oh, Miss Helen!" exclaimed Joanna. "Do look at these pretty slippers. I'm sure they would fit our wee William, and how he would love them."

"Perhaps your mother will buy them for him," said Miss Helen as she fixed on the ticket, which said £2.50.

Then Joanna and Miss Loveday took all the things they had piled on the floor and arranged them on the stall. They hung a baby's silk dress and some pretty place mats on a line at the back; then came a vase of flowers, the cushion and the workbox. And in front was the sailor's suit. In the very first row were all the boots and shoes, with the biggest football boots on the outside and Joanna's rabbitty slippers in the middle.

Joanna and Miss Loveday stood back and looked at their work. Joanna's face shone with pride as she exclaimed, "I think our stall is the nicest of all, don't you, Miss Helen?" Miss Helen could not help feeling a little proud herself.

"Well, I'm sure it's quite as nice as any of the others, Joanna." She smiled.

The next day Joanna put on her best dress with the red flowers on it, and you may be sure she was up at the village hall in good time. She found everyone adding last-minute touches to their stall, and soon all was in "apple-pie" order. On the stroke of two o'clock Joanna, Miss Loveday and all the other helpers stood ready behind their stalls. The doors were opened and the people flocked in.

Joanna noticed that a lot of the mothers made straight for their stall, and soon she was so busy serving the people and giving change that she hardly had time to see what was happening on other stalls.

Socks and boots, hats and bonnets, jumpers and skirts all disappeared, but no one bought the rabbitty slippers.

"I expect," said Joanna to herself, "that £2.50 is a lot of money for them," and she hoped that her mother would buy the slippers before anyone else did.

It was about three o'clock when there was a commotion at the door. Joanna saw Teddy Carter's mother run in looking very upset. Her hair was blown by the wind and she still had her apron tied round her waist.

"Oh dear!" she panted as the helpers hurried to her to see what was wrong. "Something dreadful has happened! My little son packed my old black skirt for your jumble sale and it has all my savings in the pocket."

"Oh please, Mrs Carter," cried Joanna, "I think I know who bought it! Don't you worry I'll soon get the money back for you." Joanna had remembered that between handing someone the baby's dress and taking the money for it, she had seen Mrs Jollyface going out of the door with a black skirt over her arm.

While everyone stood gaping at Mrs Carter in astonishment, Joanna ran out of the hall and down the road as fast as her legs could carry her. Mrs Jollyface's house was at the other end of the village, and by the time Joanna had reached the garden gate she was quite out of breath and had a stitch in her side.

Mrs Jollyface's door was ajar, and after knocking Joanna pushed it open and stepped into the kitchen. There she saw Mrs Jollyface and the twins standing quite still and staring at each other. Mrs Jollyface had an iron in one hand and several banknotes in the other. And the Jollyface twins were gazing first at the iron and then at the money and then back again.

"Well, I never!" gasped Mrs Jollyface at last. "Just look at this, Joanna! There's a lot of money in the skirt that I bought at the jumble sale. When I came to iron over the pocket I heard it crackling."

"Oh, Mrs Jollyface!" Joanna burst out. "I've come to find that money. It's Mrs Carter's and she is so worried because Teddy put the skirt in her bundle by mistake. She keeps all her savings in it."

"The poor soul!" said Mrs Jollyface. "What a state she must be in! Here, Joanna, take the skirt and money back to her. I'll put the money safe in an envelope so that you won't drop it."

Joanna thanked Mrs Jollyface, picked up the skirt and clutched the envelope tightly in the other hand.

"Please can we come with you, Joanna?" cried the Jollyface twins, who had now recovered from their surprise.

So Joanna set off for the hall with a Jollyface twin on each side of her. The twins were smaller than Joanna, not much bigger than wee William, so although the twins ran as fast as they could, Joanna only had to trot. It was just as well because she could still feel that nasty stitch in her side and she didn't think she could have run back to the hall as fast as she had come to find Mrs Jollyface.

At the village hall Mrs Carter was anxiously waiting. When she saw Joanna, Mrs Carter threw up her arms in joy. "Joanna!" she cried. "You are a fair marvel!" Then she turned to Joanna's mother and said, "There's that child, brought back all my savings, safe and sound, almost before we could turn round!"

Mother beamed at Joanna, and remarked, "Our Joanna is a good girl. When things go wrong, she can usually find a way out."

Then Mrs Carter seemed to think of something. She turned to the Jollyface twins and gave them back the black skirt. "Take that along to your mother. She bought it and she is welcome to keep it. I will send Teddy along with a jar of my tomato chutney as soon as I get home. I know your mother likes it."

"Now, Joanna," Mrs Carter continued, "I want you to choose a little present for yourself. Anything that you fancy, you shall have."

"Oh!" gasped Joanna in surprise and delight. She thought for a moment and then looked round for Miss Loveday. She went over and whispered in her ear and Miss Loveday nodded and smiled at her. Then Joanna came back to Mrs Carter and said, "I would love that pair of rabbitty slippers for wee William, but I'm afraid they cost a lot of money."

"You shall have them whatever they cost," said Mrs Carter promptly.

So Mrs Carter went to Miss Loveday's stall and Joanna watched anxiously as she looked at the price ticket. "Why, that's not dear!" she cried. "And you have saved all my savings."

The next moment, Joanna had the blue rabbitty slippers in her hand. "Look!" she cried, showing them to everyone. "Aren't they lovely and won't they suit our wee William?" And one and all agreed.

Bad Mousie

There was once a little girl called Emily who had a mouse as a pet. But he was not a good mouse; he was a bad mouse. He just loved doing naughty things! He would get Emily's scissors and start to cut up her beautiful bedspread.

You can imagine that Emily's mother was more than annoyed! She took her sweeping brush and said, "I am going to sweep you right out of our lives," and she swept him over the threshold, across the porch, down the steps and into the garden. You can imagine that Emily felt very sad.

But that night, Mousie saw a light under the door and he squeezed back into the house. Emily was so happy to see him back, but was he less bad than before?

No! He took the toilet roll and rolled it right down the stairs, through the house, until it was finished. Then, looking for something else to do, he found Emily's chalks and started to draw on the new wallpaper!

"I know what to do with you," said Emily's mother. She took a little box and put Mousie in it, tying it tightly to secure it. Then, as it was washing day, she lowered the box into the warm suds. "Good riddance," she said.

But, of course, the glue that held the box together melted in the hot water and Mousie got out and swam to the top; and there he was again back in the house! Emily was so happy that he was still there.

But he still wasn't a good Mousie. This time he tipped over the sugar and milk on the table and, not content with that, he went to Daddy's desk and upset his inkwell. The ink spread all over his papers and into the drawers below.

"I've had enough of this," said Emily's mother. "I know just what to do. I'll tie him to the fence with a yellow ribbon so that the night owl can see him clearly and gobble him up. And this is what she did.

Mousie was really scared. But Emily's mother had not reckoned with Mousie's sharp teeth, and it did not take him long to gnaw through the yellow ribbon and free himself — just in time to escape the night owl's swoop to get him.

This time he saw a window that had not been closed, and that is how he got into the house again! Emily was so relieved to see him. But he still wasn't a good Mousie; he was still a bad Mousie.

He pulled the top off the talcum powder box and spilled white powder all over the new rug. The he went to the button box, poured the buttons out and started to play with them. He also left muddy paw marks all over the house.

"This is the end. I'll get rid of you once and for all!" said Emily's mother. "Don't you know that nobody loves a bad mouse? We don't want you to stay with us any more."

It was quite hard to think of another way to get rid of bad Mousie, but she came up with a good idea: the wind would blow him away. So she got an umbrella and tied Mousie to it with string. Then she went up to the balcony and, with the first fierce gust of wind, she let go. Up and up the umbrella went until it was just a speck in the sky. Emily had a good cry.

Mousie was floating away, far away, until it touched upon a cloud and landed there. However, this was a rain cloud and soon it began to lose its drops of water, first small drops then bigger and bigger. When there were no raindrops left, Mousie started to fall down to earth. Fortunately he made a soft landing in a puddle.

Mousie had a terrible longing to go back to Emily and to a warm dry house. How he wished to become a good Mousie! He ran and ran until he reached his home and he begged Emily to teach him to be good.

Soon he learned to use scissors only for cutting out shapes, to lay the table and wipe his feet. Emily's mother was shocked at first to see Mousie back in the house but, when she saw how he did his best to be good and helpful, she was as happy as could be. And they all lived cosily together for the rest of their lives.

Susanna's Bears

Although Susanna was quite a brave girl, there was one thing she was scared of. And this one thing was bears. Not the bears in the zoo; they seemed so friendly that you could hardly be afraid of them. But the bears she could not see. And she was sure that in Auntie's linen cupboard there were several bears, because it was so warm and cosy there and it smelled nice.

Auntie Mary said, "We have no bears in our house; I would not allow it. Don't be silly!"

But Uncle John, who was for ever behind a newspaper, suddenly joined in, saying, "Bears, bears? Certainly, there is a whole family here; nice polite bears too, I seem to remember.

"How m–m–many?" Susanna asked, trembling at the very thought.

Uncle John thought for a moment. "I believe four: a Mr and Mrs and the twins."

"How do you know?"

"Well, one just knows these things. They just are, that's all."

"Don't scare Susanna," Aunt Mary said.

"She's not scared," said Uncle John, looking hard at Susanna.

She answered, "Yes, I am. I don't like bears. Just the ones in the zoo."

"These *are* the ones from the zoo," said Uncle John. "They come here at night because of the warm cupboard; their own cage is awfully chilly."

That night Susanna began to get that scary feeling again. She rushed across the landing and turned on the light in her bedroom. Then she saw an envelope propped up against her mirror with some clear writing on it. *Susanna* it said. Inside was a note, saying that the bear family would not be in that night as they were away to the hairdresser to get their hair washed and curled. *And* they were to have ice cream afterwards! Signed *Mr and Mrs Bear.*

"Well, I never!" gasped Susanna. "How can they hold pencils in these shaggy paws?" She wondered so much about this mystery that she was asleep before she knew it. The next morning she told Uncle John all about it.

"What did I tell you?" he said from behind his newspaper.

That night Susanna hurried up to her room. She no longer felt afraid of the bears and to her joy she found another letter, this time pinned to her pillow. It said:

Dear Susanna,

We will all be sound asleep when you read this, so please don't disturb us as we are very tired after our day at the zoo. We are so glad that you are staying here as we get kind of lonely at night.

The four Bs

"Imagine ..." said Susanna very softly, "bears can get lonely too." She was so quiet so as not to waken them that she fell sound asleep in no time at all.

Next morning Susanna asked Uncle John, "Do you think they like staying at the zoo? Perhaps they would rather be here all the time."

He answered, "They probably would but, you see, unless they belong to someone special, they have to stay at the zoo."

"How I wish they belonged to me," said Susanna.

That night she absolutely rushed upstairs. An envelope was pinned to her chair.

Dear Susanna,

We like you so much that we do wish we could belong to you. The zoo is all right but we like it better here. If we could belong to you, look behind the airing cupboard door. We will be waiting for you.

The four Bs

Susanna hurried across the landing and opened the door. There in the airing cupboard were four bears: a big one, a medium one and two little ones the same size.

"Oh, you darlings!" Susanna shouted, and gathered them up in her arms.

"You can sleep beside me tonight." She tucked them in cosily and all of them were asleep together in the bed in no time at all.

The next morning she brushed them all neatly and carried them down.

"Here are the bear family. They got tired of the zoo and they wanted to be my very own bears."

"Delighted to meet you," said Uncle John, making a bow.

"Oh, Uncle John!" Susanna cried. "Thank you so much; I just love my bears. Wasn't I silly to be afraid?"

The Seven Ravens

There was once a father and mother who had seven children. They were all boys and the parents longed for a daughter. Now, one day their wish was granted and a beautiful baby girl was born to them. But she looked poorly and it seemed as if she might not have long to live. So the parents were anxious to baptise her as soon as possible. They needed water to baptise the child and so they gave their sons a jug to collect water from the well.

Well, you know what boys are like; they were running and shouting: "I want to carry the jug!" "No, I want to as I'm the eldest!" "But I'm the strongest!" "No, me, I'm the quickest!"

In the excitement they forgot to be careful, and can you guess what happened?

The jug went from hand to hand and inevitably it fell and was broken into a thousand pieces.

Of course the boys were very upset, and they went home with hanging heads and dragging feet carrying the pieces.

Naturally the parents were cross, and the father said in a moment of anger, "You awful boys. I just wish you would turn into ravens!"

No sooner had he said this than the boys began to change. Their noses turned into beaks, their hair into feathers, their legs into bony bird's legs and their arms into wings. They flew off in a flock of seven and were never seen again.

How the father regretted his words and, to his despair, his curse could only be removed by an act of great love.

Contrary to expectations, the baby lived and grew into a beautiful, and also good, little girl, in whom the father and mother found great comfort.

However, the girl noticed that sometimes people whispered to each other when they saw her in the village, and soon she found out what they were saying: "You seen that little girl there? Well, she has seven brothers who were turned into ravens and it's all her fault."

How shocked she was! She ran home and asked her parents, "Is it true that I have brothers, seven of them?"

The father and mother looked at each other and answered, "Yes, it is true."

"And were they turned into birds, into ravens?"

Again the father and mother looked at each other and said, "Yes, it is true."

"And is it my fault?"

"No, that is not true." And they explained to the girl what had happened.

It was not long before the girl said, "I am going to find my brothers."

The father and mother tried to dissuade her but she was determined. All she wanted to take with her was a jug of water in case she got thirsty, a loaf of bread and a little stool to rest on if she should get tired. Her mother gave her one of her rings and as the girl left home she put it on her finger.

After saying goodbye to her parents, the girl set off, carrying the jug, the loaf of bread and the little stool. She went to the North and South, to the East and West and nowhere could she find her brothers who had been turned into ravens. The loaf of bread was soon finished, so was the water in the jug and she was getting very, very tired. She used the little stool more and more often.

At last she came to the end of the world. Then she thought, "I shall ask the moon. He moves across the sky and he is sure to know where my brothers are."

But the moon was unkind and said only, "No, I haven't seen them."

Then she asked the sun. The sun was more kind and said, "I'm sorry that I have not met your brothers, but why don't you ask the stars? There are so many of them; they could work together and surely one of them may have noticed your brothers."

This is what she did and, yes, it was the evening star that came forward and said, "I believe I have seen them. They live with an old dwarf in a glass mountain; why don't you try there?"

It did not take her long until she saw in the far distance this strangely built house of glass. When she reached it, she knocked. The door was opened by a dwarf with a kind face. She enquired about her brothers who were now ravens and he answered, "Why, yes, they do live here. They are out at the moment but I expect them back soon for their supper. You can wait here for them." The dwarf showed her into a room where the table was set for seven: seven plates and seven goblets. The girl took her mother's ring off her finger and put it into one of the deep glasses. And then she hid behind the door.

Soon there was a gust of air, a fluttering of wings and one after the other the birds flew in. They settled themselves around the table and then one of them saw the glitter of the ring. He picked it out carefully with his beak and, showing it to the others, said, "Do you recognize this ring?"

Some answered right away, "Yes, yes, it's our mother's ring. How did it get here? Perhaps the time has come when we can return to our human form. Perhaps someone has come to rescue us!"

When the girl heard this she could no longer hide herself, and she came forward, saying, "I have come to take you home."

They embraced their sister and as the girl touched each one in turn, through the power of love, they began to change: their beaks became noses, their feathers became hair, their wings became arms and their bird legs became human legs. They said goodbye to the dwarf and thanked him for looking after them so well and then they walked home together.

You can imagine how happy the father and mother were to see not only their beautiful daughter safely back, but also their seven sons whom they thought were lost for ever. And they all lived happily ever after.

The Lion and the Mouse

King Lion was lying fast asleep. He had no enemies but man and his tummy was full. He was having a wonderful dream about chasing antelopes, and the tip of his tail was twitching with excitement. Unknown to him, a tiny mouse was watching this and, fascinated by the movement, sprang as if catching prey.

This woke the lion up and, in a moment, he pounced and held the mouse in his mighty paw, ready to crush him with his huge teeth.

"Oh please, King Lion, dear King Lion, spare me. I meant you no harm. I was just playing. Besides, I am so small that you would hardly taste me."

"Oh no," said King Lion. "He who annoys the king shall pay for it."

"Please, please have mercy on me. Who knows, I may save your life one day."

At this the king laughed heartily, saying, "I very much doubt that." But he let the mouse go.

Now, it was some months later that the mouse got his chance.

As I mentioned before, the lion's only enemy was man, and there were those who had hunted him many times and in many ways. As this lion lived in a forest, the hunters decided to make a trap for him. They dug a deep pit and covered it with a net and then branches and leaves, so that no one but the hunters could see that there was danger. And this is exactly what happened. The King of the Beasts stepped on the trap and it collapsed. The lion fell in with a great roar. He became entangled in the net and could not get out.

And who heard the roar?

The mouse, of course. He thought, "My friend the lion is in danger. I must go to his aid." And so, as fast as his little legs would carry him, he ran and ran until he found the source of the noise.

"Oh King, I have come to help you. You saved my life and now it is time for me to save yours."

If the circumstances had not been so serious the lion would have laughed. "How on earth?" was all he could say.

But the mouse answered, "I have very sharp teeth. Now, don't talk to me. I have work to do."

Carefully the mouse stepped on to the net and began to chew. Soon there was quite a big hole in the net, but not big enough to let the lion out. It was getting dark and the mouse knew that the hunters would soon be back to see what was in their trap. He redoubled his efforts and chewed and chewed, until before long the hole was big enough to let the lion squeeze out. Just then they heard the hunters coming nearer.

"Quick, on my back," said the lion. And so the two escaped. And they stayed friends for the rest of their lives. And, to this day, a lion will never harm a mouse.

The Story of Beth

Once upon a time there was a little girl called Beth, who lived with her grandmother as both her parents had died. They lived in a small wooden house in the forest. They loved each other dearly and were very happy together. One day each week they walked to the nearby village. They each carried a basket: Grandma the bigger and Beth the smaller.

One day when they set out it was bitterly cold and Grandma said, "This is just the sort of cold that comes before snow. I don't think it can be far away so we'd better not linger in case we get caught in a snowstorm.

Well, that is just what happened. Because they lived in the forest and hardly ever met anyone, it was so nice to chat and hear all the news and to choose their shopping slowly and carefully. So they stayed longer in the village than they had meant to.

At last they set off home. By now the sky was very dark and heavy and it felt as though a great blanket would fall on top of them. Granny and Beth walked as fast as they could, but the old woman could not keep up with the young girl. "Please, Beth, not so fast," she pleaded.

Then the first snowflakes started to form, at first tiny then larger until soon they came so thick and fast that, had they not known the forest so well, they might have lost their way.

Granny started to cough and to fall behind. When Beth noticed, she walked back and took Granny's basket and supported her with her arm.

"I can't go on," sighed the old woman.

"Yes you can, we're almost there," said Beth. And she went on talking to Granny about the fire she would light (Wasn't it all set and only needed a match?), the soup she would warm, and how soft and cosy her bed would be.

How long it seemed to the house, although they must be quite near now. Grandma leaned more heavily on Beth's arm. She stopped every now and then to cough and to sigh, and to Beth the two baskets were becoming unbearably heavy, not to mention Granny leaning heavily on her.

"How I would like to play with the snow fairies," thought Beth.

When they at last arrived at the cottage, Beth saw to everything: to the fire, to hot soup for her granny after she had tucked her up in bed with a hot water bottle.

Beth did not go out until Granny was fast asleep. Then Beth went to the door and looked out. By now it was dark outside but the thick covering of snow made everything look clean and beautiful. She thought of other children who were free to go out and play in the snow. It was getting colder and colder. As she stood there, Beth could not help but cry a little, and the salt tears fell on the snow and melted it.

Next day the sun shone and made everything look like Fairyland.

"Off you go," said Granny. "I am better now, thanks to you, dear child. The snow fairies are still there waiting for you to come out and play."

Beth wrapped up warmly, and when she stepped out of the door where she had stood the night before feeling so sad, she saw something she had not noticed before. There at her feet a plant had grown right through the snow and on its branches hung a cluster of white flowers. She gently picked some and took them into Grandma.

Grandma thanked Beth and smiled. "There now, that's your reward from the fairies for looking after others before pleasing yourself."

The flower was a Christmas rose, and it came back every Christmas thereafter.

Erwin the Elf

Once upon a time there was a family who lived in the country. In their home they had many old-fashioned pieces of furniture, like a grandfather clock, chests bound with copper and four-poster beds. They also had a Welsh dresser — a cupboard that usually has drawers below and shelves above on which people display their favourite pieces of china.

On the top shelf of this Welsh dresser stood a row of blue and white cups. To ordinary people's eyes, these cups looked all the same, but they were not all the same. One of them was special. In it lived an elf called Erwin; it was his home and it was where he slept when he was not busy.

But nobody knew this!

Until one day when Mother burned the soup. Nobody could eat it because it tasted horrible. Mother set the pan to soak overnight and the next day she scrubbed and scrubbed to try to get it clean again. She managed to get some of the burned soup off, but the rest was so stubborn that she almost decided to throw the pan away. Almost, but not quite ...

Because, guess what happened?

Next morning Mother went to get her pan. It was one of her favourites and she felt sad to part with it. And when she looked, it was clean! Not just ordinary clean but spanking clean! She could not understand it and she called Father and the children, wondering if perhaps they had done it.

But no! They had not. It was a mystery.

The next strange thing happened when mother was sewing new curtains. It was late at night and she was getting tired. By accident she dropped a whole box of pins on the floor, and there they were, all over the place. "I'll pick them up tomorrow when the light is better," she muttered to herself.

But the next morning, when she went to put the pins back in their box, there they were, all picked up, not a single one left on the floor, and the lid put back on the box.

Everyone was puzzled: who had done this good deed?

And then Father said, "I do believe we have an elf in the house — a kind elf who wants to help us"

"Where, where?" cried the children. Oh how much they wanted to see their good friend. But no one can see an elf, and no one can hear an elf. You can only see one when it wants to be seen or heard.

And all the time, Erwin the elf was watching them over the brim of the blue and white cup on the top shelf of the Welsh dresser.

Several more unexplained things happened to that family until, one day, Mother said, "You know, we ought to thank this elf for his good deeds."

But how?

There were all sorts of suggestions, and finally they came to the idea of making a pie for him.

"What shall we fill it with?" asked one of the children.

"Blueberries, of course; there are plenty just now."

So they set to and made a scrumptious pie and left it on the kitchen table with a short note: *Thank you dear elf for helping us!*

The next morning they were up early to see if the elf had liked their present. It was all gone! How could a wee elf eat so much?

And all the time Erwin was watching them from his blue and white cup on the Welsh dresser, with smears of blueberry on his cheeks and his tummy all round and distended.

Well, time went on and sometimes Erwin weeded a row of carrots or mended a tear in someone's trousers. And the family wanted once more to thank the elf. But the time for blueberries was past and so they made a cherry pie this time.

To their great surprise it remained totally untouched. Perhaps he was on holiday? Or perhaps he did not like cherries! Oh dear, what to do?

"We must try different fruits in the pie," said Mother. What else was ready in their own garden?

Rhubarb, of course, but that was too sour.

Gooseberries then: too prickly.

Strawberries: not quite ripe yet.

Aaah! Raspberries: ripe and sweet.

Everybody helped: Father was good at pastry; the sisters picked and weighed the fruit; Mother set the oven at the right temperature; and the boys insisted that they would wash up and clear everything away. Soon they could smell the pie all through the house. It was left on the table on a clean white tablecloth.

They could hardly wait until the next morning.

As soon as it was light, they bounced downstairs straight to the kitchen. They could see from a distance that there had been a disturbance around the plate. It really looked a mess at first, but they soon saw it wasn't.

It was a message!

The elf must have gobbled up the pie and then tramped with great joy in the red juice: there were his wee footsteps all over the white tablecloth. It was as if he had skates on: words slid and slithered all over the place, but you could clearly see that they said:

THANK YOU!

Borka

Once upon a time there were two geese called Mr and Mrs Plumster. They lived in the quiet countryside in England where their family had always lived. There they built their nest and laid their eggs. Each spring the Plumsters came back to the marshes and mended their nest. Then Mrs Plumster settled down to lay her eggs and Mr Plumster kept guard. He hissed at anything that came near the nest. Sometimes he hissed even when there was nothing in sight; it made him feel important. Then the eggs began to hatch.

One fine spring morning there were six plump baby Plumsters in the nest. Mr Plumster was delighted and invited his friends round to celebrate. The young geese were given names. They were Archie, Frieda, Jennifer, Oswald, Timothy and Borka.

Now all geese look very much alike when they are young, but right from the start there was something odd about Borka. She had a beak, wings and webbed feet like all her brothers and sisters but she did not have any feathers. Mr and Mrs Plumster were very worried about this. They called in the doctor goose, who came along with his little leather bag.

The doctor examined Borka carefully and said that there was nothing wrong with her except that she did not have any feathers. And he said it was a most unusual case. He thought for a long while, then he told Mrs Plumster that there was only one thing to do: she must knit some feathers for Borka.

So Mrs Plumster got out her knitting needles and set to work. Of course she could not knit real feathers, but she made a kind of grey woollen jersey, as much like feathers as she could. When she had finished she called Borka and tried it on her.

Borka was delighted and flapped around with joy because she had always felt chilly at night. She went and showed the other young geese, but they just laughed at her. This made her very unhappy and she went into a patch of tall reeds and cried.

By this time, the other young geese were learning to fly and to swim properly. But Borka did not like joining in because the others teased her and so she got very behind with her lessons. Nobody noticed that she was not attending. Mr and Mrs Plumster were far too busy. Borka did try to learn to swim, but whenever she went in the water, her jersey took such a long time to dry afterwards that she soon gave up.

By now the summer was almost over. The weather was getting cooler and the geese were becoming restless. At this time of year they always flew to a warmer land, where it was easier to find food. The Plumsters began to get ready to leave. They covered their nest with twigs and rushes to keep it safe through the stormy winter.

Then one day it became really cold and wet. The geese shivered and knew that it was time for them to go. They chose one wise old goose to lead them and they all flew away. But Borka did not go. She could not fly. Instead, she hid and watched them leave. No one noticed that she was missing. They were all too busy thinking of the journey ahead.

As the geese disappeared into the grey sky, tears trickled down Borka's beak. She did not know what to do. It was drizzling and she wandered off, hoping to find a dry place for the night.

It was already getting dark when she came to a line of boats moored in the estuary. Borka chose one that had no lights on board and she walked up the gangplank. She was just going down into the hold of the boat when there was loud bark. A dog came rushing out, which gave Borka a terrible fright.

But the dog, seeing that it was only a goose, stopped barking and introduced himself. He was called Fowler. Borka explained that she only wanted to stay under cover for the night, so Fowler showed her into a part of the hold where there were some old sacks for her to lie on.

Now, the boat, which was called the Crombie, belonged to Captain Alisdair. Late that night he and his mate, whose name was Fred, came back and decided to set sail next morning before it was light. Fowler forgot all about Borka, who was still asleep in the hold. It was not until they were well on their way that he remembered and told the Captain.

"Well, well!" said Captain Alisdair. " A goose on board. She will have to work her passage if she is coming with us to London."

Borka was soon very friendly with the Captain, Fred and, of course, with Fowler. She coiled lengths of rope with her beak, picked up crumbs from the floor and helped in any way she could. In return, she was given plenty of good food. At last the Crombie steered into the River Thames and they were nearing London.

Captain Alisdair wondered what to do with Borka when they got there. He decided to leave her in Kew Gardens. This is a large park where lots of geese live all the year round. When they came to the place where the river flows past Kew Gardens, Captain Alisdair lifted Borka over the railings and put her with the other geese. She was sorry to say goodbye to her friends. They promised to visit her on their next trip to London.

The geese at Kew did not mind that Borka had no feathers. There were already so many strange birds in the gardens. Nobody laughed at her grey woollen jersey, and all the geese were very friendly, especially one called Ferdinand. Ferdinand cared for Borka and taught her to swim really well.

She is still living there happily, and whenever Captain Alisdair, Fred and Fowler come to London, they call in to see her. So if you are in Kew Gardens at any time and you see a goose that looks somehow different from the others, it might well be Borka.

Granny Glittens and her Amazing Mittens

Once upon a time there was an old lady who lived in a village. Her name was Mrs Glittens but everybody called her Granny Glittens. She was a tremendous knitter. There was nothing she liked more than sitting down in her rocking chair beside the fire, the cat keeping her company, knitting as though her life depended on it.

Her speciality was knitting mittens. Each year she knitted the most beautiful mittens in all the colours of the rainbow for the children in her village. She got so well known that their parents ordered mittens well before Christmas, specifying a colour that suited their little boys or girls. Usually the old mittens were lost or worn out, so it was always a pleasant surprise to get a new pair.

Well, one particular autumn, when the nights started to draw in and it was getting colder, Granny Gittens began to think about knitting new mittens for the children of the village. She got out her knitting needles and then she walked over to the drawer in the cupboard in the kitchen where she kept the coloured wool. But, oh dear, what a shock she got! There were only a few strands of coloured wool left and masses and masses of white wool! That would never do: just white mittens are rather boring, and besides, they get dirty so quickly.

So she sat down to write a letter to the wool supplier to order all the colours of wool that she would like to start her yearly knit. Quite soon an answer came back:

Dear Granny Glittens,

We are sorry to inform you that we no longer do a line in coloured wool but we will be pleased to send you the usual amount in white wool of excellent quality.

Oh dear, that would never do! But quite soon a large box arrived from the factory, full of white balls of fluffy white wool. Granny Glittens was very upset. What was she to do?

She decided to comfort herself with a nice warm cup of cocoa. As she opened her store cupboard she was faced with a row of glass jars. There was chocolate, of course, but also sweets of all sorts like blue peppermints, old-fashioned wintergreens, raspberry lozenges, light and dark brown liquorice, yellow butter sweets and many more.

Suddenly a thought came to her ... Oh no, that would never be possible ... What about giving it a try!

She completely forgot about her warm drink and got out all her pans. She filled the pans with warm water and dropped in some sweets. The resulting colour was a bit too weak and so she added more until she had the desired strength. Then she dipped in her white wool. The result was amazing: slowly but surely the white wool took on a lovely new range of colours. It took a long, long time and a lot of sweets to dye the huge quantity of wool. Then it all had to hang somewhere to dry. How cheerful her house looked with the fluffy coloured wool hanging everywhere.

At long last the moment arrived when Granny Glittens could start to knit. It was awkward at first as the wool was kind of stiff and sticky. But she soon got the hang of it. When Granny licked her fingers they had a really nice taste.

In came the orders for the Christmas mittens: red for Johnny, blue for Jane, green for Clare, brown for James and so on and so on.

On Christmas morning when the children opened their presents they were really surprised: they could hardly get their fingers into the right places because the mittens were so stiff! It didn't take them long to find out that they not only smelled, but also tasted delicious and all too soon all the mittens were eaten! It was too good to be true.

The next year Granny Glittens got more orders than ever for mittens, but mostly for mittens that could be eaten with a fork and knife!

Stories for Children
Aged Six to Seven

King of the Birds

You all know, of course, who the King of the Beasts is, don't you? Yes, of course, it is the lion. He has no enemies but man. He is strong and clever and you can see by the way he walks that he knows he is very important.

Well, one day some birds were talking together and one said, "How come the beasts have a king and we do not?"

"You are right," said another. "We shall have to do something about that! What do you suggest? Any ideas?"

Well, believe it or not, it was the common sparrow, the bird we all know so well that we don't think they are at all special, who came up with a splendid idea.

"Why don't we all line up somewhere, and at a signal we start flying, and the bird who gets nearest the sun could be pronounced king?"

What an excellent idea! No bird could think of anything better.

"But where shall we do this?" asked the magpie.

"Not in a wood for a start," said the blackbird, "because the trees may get in the way."

And the robin said, "And not on too hot a day, as we shall get tired too quickly."

Well, after many suggestions they decided on an open field that faced south and that every bird knew. It was not too far away for any bird to get to.

Now, they had to find someone to judge the competition. It ought to be a bird, but not one of the competitors. Perhaps a bird that was not a very good flier or one who did not want to be in the competition.

"I know," said the pigeon, "the owl; he only flies at night and he is very wise." The owl was asked, and he was awfully pleased to be considered important enough to judge this very special occasion.

Well, as the day drew nearer the birds talked about nothing else; they were all so excited and practised flying high. On the day itself the weather was brilliant without a cloud in the sky. Most birds were in the field early and were already flapping their wings.

And here was the owl! He had put on a pair of dark spectacles because it was daylight and it also made him look extra wise! He at once began organising the birds into a straight line.

"Now, no cheating," said the owl. "Leave room for your neighbour to spread his wings! You are familiar with the object of this race? You fly as high as you can, and the one who gets nearest the sun will be King of the Birds! Now, ready, steady, go!"

After a few false starts, the race really got going.

The little wren piped up, "I'm going to be the king!"

But the eagle answered, "Don't be ridiculous; your wings are far too small."

Quite soon the smaller birds fell back. First the blue tits and robins; then the sparrows and magpies and pigeons and even the jackdaws and hawks could not keep up. Only the really strong birds, the ravens and buzzards and vultures still soared up and up. But way ahead of them was the eagle and, try as they might, they could not catch him up.

At last it was just the golden eagle that was in the sky. But even he got tired and could not go higher. So he called down to the others, "Of all birds, I am nearest to the sun and so I shall be called King. Where are you now, little Jenny Wren?"

From beneath the eagle's thick, strong feathers flew out a tiny bird, a little Jenny Wren who had been hiding there. And she flew higher and higher until she got so close to the sun that it scorched the feathers on her head. It looked just like a little golden crown.

And so it was that the eagle, on coming down exhausted, admitted he had been tricked by clever Jenny Wren and that he could not be crowned King of the Birds. And, as it was, the wren was already wearing the crown. This special bird is called the golden crested wren.

So, you see, it is not always the biggest that is best. Remember that!

How the Zebra Got its Stripes

When God first created all the animals, he did not give them any colours; they were all still white. Then God called his angels and said, "Here are jars of paint and brushes. You call the animals and paint colours on them as they come."

The angels called the animals out and got busy with their paints and brushes. Some of them liked to paint a lot of different colours on them: the parrot, for instance, was painted red and green and yellow; the peacock was painted blue and gold; the tiger wanted yellow fur and black stripes, and the giraffe wanted brown patches. Other animals wanted just one colour: the lion yellow, the elephant grey and the frog green. Some, like the polar bear, said, "I live all the year round in snow and ice; I would rather stay white."

So the angels painted the animals as they came along. And they used up all the paints until only one jar of black paint was left. They said, "We hope there are no more animals to be painted; we have no colours left, only black!"

Then one angel said, "Oh dear, look! There are still two zebras trotting and galloping outside. They've been playing about while all the others were being painted and they are still quite white!" All the angels started to shout, "Zebras, zebras! Come here, you naughty creatures. Don't you want to be painted?"

The zebras came running and said, "Oh, yes please, we don't want to stay white. We would like to get a colour too! Could we please be painted red and blue and orange and green?"

"I'm so sorry," said one of the angels. "None of these colours are left; there's only black. And, you know, there's really only enough left for one of you."

"Then paint me black," said one of the zebras. "I'm not going to stay white."

"No, paint me," said the other. "I don't want to stay white!"

"No, ME!" "No, ME!" They nearly started a fight there and then, but the angels stopped them just in time.

"Listen," said one of the angels, "there's not enough paint for both of you so, to be quite fair, I can paint half of both of you. How would you like to have one side white and the other black? Or the front white and the back black? Which would you prefer?"

"No!" shrieked the first zebra. "I don't want to be half black, whether it's left or right or front or back!" And the other zebra said just the same.

At last the Angel said, "You silly creatures; if only you had listened when we called all the animals and had come straight away, we wouldn't have had all this nonsense. Now, listen. I'm going to give you each some nice black stripes and there's an end to it."

"Yes, yes!" cried the two zebras. "Give us black stripes! We like black stripes!"

And that is how the zebra got its stripes.

How the Elephant Got its Trunk

Long, long ago, elephants had no trunk. They only had a very big, fat nose, rather like a boot, and they could not pick anything up with that.

Now, there was once a young elephant who was very, very curious about things and he was always full of questions. He asked all the other animals so many things that they became quite cross with him, and the only way to stop him was to smack him. He asked the ostrich why her feathers grew all fluffy and were no use for flying. And the ostrich smacked him with her hard, hard claw. Then he asked the giraffe why his coat was so spotty. And he smacked him with his hard hoof. He asked the hippopotamus why her eyes were so red. And she smacked him with her hard, hard hoof. Then he asked the baboon why he was so hairy. And he smacked him with his hairy, hairy paw. But the smacking did not help a bit. The young elephant was still full of curiosity. He asked questions about everything he saw, or heard, or felt, or smelled, or touched. And everybody smacked him. But still he was curious.

One fine morning this elephant child asked a new question that he had never asked before: "What does the crocodile have for dinner?"

Everybody said, "Hush!" in a very loud voice, and they smacked him immediately and didn't stop for a long time.

Then one day he met a Kolo Kolo bird sitting in the middle of a thorn bush, and he said, "Everybody smacks me because of my curiosity, but I still want to know what a crocodile has for dinner."

The Kolo Kolo bird said, "Go to the banks of the great, grey-green, greasy, Limpopo River, all set about with fever trees, and there you will find out."

The very next morning the elephant child took a hundred pounds of bananas and a hundred pounds of sugar cane and seventeen melons and said goodbye to all his dear family. "I am going to the great, grey-green, greasy, Limpopo River, all set about with fever trees to find out what the crocodile has for dinner." And they all smacked him once more for luck, though he asked them most politely to stop.

Then he went off, eating melons and throwing the rinds away because he could not pick them up. He carried on his way until at last he came to the great, grey-green, greasy, Limpopo River, all set about with fever trees, exactly as the Kolo Kolo bird had said.

Now, remember that this young elephant had never seen a crocodile, so he did not know what it looked like. So when he saw a python snake curled around a rock the elephant said, "'Scuse me, have you seen a crocodile here-abouts?"

The snake answered, "What a question? Any more?"

"Yes, what does he have for dinner?"

Then the snake uncoiled himself and smacked the Elephant with his tail.

"That is strange. Everybody smacks me because of my curiosity!" the elephant said. So he said goodbye to the snake and went on, until he stepped on what he thought was a log at the edge of the great Limpopo River. But it was really a crocodile and he winked with one eye like this.

"'Scuse me, have you perhaps seen a crocodile around here?" said the young elephant.

Then the crocodile winked with the other eye and lifted half his tail out of the mud. The elephant stepped back politely because he did not want to be smacked again.

The crocodile said, "Come to me, for I am a crocodile." And he wept crocodile tears to show that it was true.

The young elephant kneeled down on the bank and said, "You are the very person I've been looking for all these long days. Will you tell me what you have for dinner?"

"Come closer," said the crocodile, "and I'll whisper it in your ear."

The elephant put his head down close to the musky, tusky mouth, and the crocodile caught him by the nose which, up to that very week, day, hour and minute, had been no bigger than a boot.

"I think," said the crocodile between his teeth, "I think, today, I shall begin with young elephant!"

At this the elephant got very annoyed and he said, "Let go, you're hurting me!"

At that moment the python snake slid down the bank and said, "My friend, if you do not now, immediately and instantly, pull as hard as you can, it's my opinion that this animal will pull you into the river."

So the elephant sat back on its haunches and pulled and pulled, and his nose began to stretch. And the crocodile floundered in the water, and he pulled and pulled, and the elephant's nose kept on stretching. The baby elephant spread all four legs and he pulled and pulled, and his nose kept on stretching. The crocodile thrashed his tail like an oar, and he pulled and pulled, and at each pull the elephant baby's nose got longer and longer. And it hurt awfully!

Then the elephant felt his legs slipping and he said through his nose, which was now nearly five feet long, "This is too much for me!"

The python snake came down from the bank and knotted itself around the elephant's hind legs and said, "We will work together or you will end up in the crocodile's tummy." So he pulled, and the baby elephant pulled, and the crocodile pulled. But the elephant and the snake pulled hardest, and at last the crocodile let go of the elephant's nose with a loud plop that you could hear all the way up and down the Limpopo River.

Then the baby elephant sat down, but not before saying thank you to the snake. Then he looked after his poor stretched nose and wrapped it all up in banana leaves and hung it in the river to cool.

"Why are you doing that?" asked the snake.

"'Scuse me," the baby elephant answered, "but my nose is badly hurt and I'm waiting for it to shrink."

The snake said, "Then you will have to wait for a very long time. Besides, the crocodile might come back."

The elephant sat there for three whole days waiting for his nose to shrink but it never grew any shorter. At the end of the third day a fly came and stung him on the shoulder, and before he knew what he was doing he had lifted up his new trunk and hit the fly with the end of it.

"Well done!" said the snake. "Now, you couldn't have done that before, could you? Now try to eat a little."

Before he knew what he was doing the baby elephant had put out his trunk and plucked a large bundle of grass, dusted it clean against his forelegs and put it into his mouth.

"Bravo!" cried the snake. "Hey, don't you think the sun is very hot here?"

"It is," said the elephant, and before he knew what he was doing he scooped up some mud from the Limpopo River and slapped it on his head, where it made a lovely cool mud-pack, all trickly behind his ears.

The snake cried, "Another advantage of having a long nose! Now, how do you feel about being smacked again?"

"I shouldn't like it at all," answered the young elephant.

"How would *you* like to smack somebody?" said the snake.

The elephant answered, "I should like it very much indeed."

"Well," said the python, "you will find that long nose of yours very handy to smack people with."

"Good," said the elephant. "I think I'll go home now to all my dear family and try it out!"

So the baby elephant walked home across Africa, frisking and whisking his trunk. When he wanted fruit to eat he pulled it down from a tree instead of waiting for it to fall as he used to do. When he wanted grass he plucked it from the ground instead of going down on his knees as he used to do. When flies annoyed him he broke a branch from a tree and used it as a fly swat, and he made himself a new, cool, slushy-squashy mud-cap whenever the sun was hot. When he felt lonely walking through Africa, he sang to himself down his trunk and the sound was louder than several brass bands. The rest of the time he picked up the melon rinds that he had dropped on his way to the Limpopo River, for he was a tidy elephant.

One dark evening he arrived back to all his dear family and he coiled up his trunk and said, "How do you do."

They were overjoyed to see him and said, "Come here and be smacked for your curiosity."

"Who?" said the baby elephant. "I don't think you know anything about smacking." Then he uncurled his new trunk and knocked two of his brothers head over heels.

"Oh, bananas!" they said. "Where did you learn that trick and what have you done to your nose?"

"I got a new one from the crocodile on the banks of the great, grey-green, greasy Limpopo River, all set about with fever trees. I asked him what he had for dinner and he gave me this to keep."

"It looks very ugly," said his hairy uncle the baboon.

"Perhaps so, but it's very useful," answered the elephant, and he picked up his hairy uncle the baboon by one hairy leg and threw him into an ants' nest. He pulled out his tall ostrich aunt's tail feathers and he caught his tall uncle, the giraffe, by the hind leg and dragged him through a thorn bush. He shouted at his broad aunt the hippopotamus and blew bubbles into her ear when she was sleeping in the water after a meal; but he never let anyone touch the Kolo Kolo bird.

His elephant family were so impressed by the usefulness of the trunk that he had got from the crocodile that they went off one by one in a hurry to the banks of the great, grey-green, greasy Limpopo River, all set about with fever trees, to get new noses for themselves. When they came back, all with their brand-new trunks, nobody smacked anybody any more.

And ever since that day, all the elephants that you will ever see, besides all those you won't, have trunks precisely like the trunk of the curious young elephant.

The Cat Who Walked Alone

This all happened when the tame animals were wild. The dog was wild, the horse was wild, the cow was wild and the sheep was wild. The pig was wild as wild could be, and they all walked in the wet, wild woods. But the cat was the wildest of them all; he walked by himself and all places were alike to him.

Of course, the man was wild too. He was dreadfully wild. He didn't even begin to be tame until he met the woman and she told him that she did not like living in his wild ways. She picked out a nice, dry cave instead of a heap of wet leaves to lie down on, and she strewed clean sand on the floor, and she lit a nice fire of wood at the back of the cave, and she hung a dried wild horse-skin, tail down, across the opening of the cave, and she said, "Wipe your feet, dear, when you come in, and now we shall keep house."

That night they ate wild sheep on hot stones, flavoured with wild garlic and wild pepper. They also ate wild duck stuffed with wild rice and wild fenugreek and wild coriander. As well as all that, there were marrow bones from wild oxen with wild cherries. After his feast the man went to sleep in front of the fire feeling ever so happy. But the woman sat up combing her hair. She took the bone from a shoulder of mutton — the big flat blade bone — and she looked at the wonderful marks on it. She threw more wood on the fire. Then she made a magic spell. It was the first singing magic spell in the whole wide world.

Out in the wet, wild woods all the wild animals gathered where they could see the light of the fire a long way off, and they wondered what it meant. Then the wild horse stamped his wild foot and said, "Oh, my friends and oh, my enemies, why have the man and the woman made that great light in that great cave and what harm will it do us?"

The wild dog lifted up his wild nose and smelled the smell of roast mutton and said, "I will go up and see and look and say, for I think it is good. Cat, come with me!"

"Miaouw," said the cat. "I am the cat who walks alone. I will not come."

The wild dog answered, "Then we can never be friends again," and he trotted off to the cave.

But when he had gone a little way the cat said to himself, "Why should I not go too and come away at my own liking?" So he slipped after the wild dog softly, very softly, and hid himself where he could hear everything.

When the wild dog reached the mouth of the cave, he lifted up the dry horse-skin with his nose and sniffed the beautiful smell of the roast mutton. The woman, looking at the blade bone, heard him and laughed and said, "Here comes the first wild thing of the wild woods. What do you want?"

The wild dog said, "What is this that smells so good in the wild woods?"

Then the woman picked up a roast mutton bone and threw it to the wild dog and said, "Wild thing out of the wild woods, taste and try."

The wild dog gnawed the bone and it was more delicious than anything he had ever tasted. He said, "Please give me another."

The woman said, "Wild thing of the wild woods, help my man to hunt through the day and guard this cave at night, and I will give you as many roast bones as you like."

"Ah, this is a very wise woman, but she is not as wise as I am," said the cat, listening.

The wild dog crawled into the cave and laid his head on the woman's lap and said, "Oh, my friend, I will help your man to hunt during the day and at night I will guard your cave."

The cat said, listening, "That is a very foolish dog." And the cat went back to the wet, wild woods waving his wild tail and walking by his lonely self. But he never told anybody.

When the man woke up, he said, "What is the wild dog doing here?"

The woman answered, "His name is not Wild Dog any more but First Friend, because he will be our friend for always and always and always. Take him with you when you go hunting."

Next day the woman cut great armfuls of fresh, green grass from the water-meadows and dried it before the fire so that it smelled like new-mown hay, and she sat at the mouth of the cave and plaited a halter out of horse-hide, and she looked at the shoulder of mutton bone — at the big broad blade bone — and she made another magic spell. She made the second singing magic spell in the whole wide world.

Out in the wild woods all the wild animals wondered what had happened to the wild dog and, at last, the wild horse stamped his foot and said, "I will go and see why the wild dog has not returned. Cat, come with me."

"Miaouw," said the cat. I am the cat who walks alone. I will not come with you." But, all the same, he followed the wild horse very, very softly and hid himself where he could hear everything.

When the woman heard the wild horse tripping and stumbling on his long mane, she laughed and said, "Here comes the second thing out of the wild woods. What do you want?"

The wild horse said, " Where is the wild dog?"

The woman laughed and picked up the blade bone and looked at it and said, "Wild thing out of the wild woods, you did not come here for the wild dog but for the sake of this good grass."

And the wild horse, tripping and stumbling on his mane, said, "That is true. Give it to me to eat."

"Wild thing out of the wild woods, bend your wild head and wear what I give you, and you shall eat this wonderful grass three times a day."

"Ah, this is a clever woman, but she is not so clever as I am," said the listening cat.

The wild horse bent his wild head and the woman slipped the plaited hide halter over it. The wild horse breathed on the woman's feet and said, "Oh, my mistress, I will be your servant for the sake of the wonderful grass."

"Ah, this is a very foolish horse," said the cat, listening. And he went back to the wet, wild woods, waving his wild tail and walking alone. But he never told anybody.

When the man and the dog came back from hunting, the man said, "What is this wild horse doing here?"

And the woman answered, "His name is not Wild Horse any more but First Servant, because he will carry us from place to place for always and always and always. And you can ride on his back when you go hunting."

Next day, holding her wild head high so that her wild horns would not get caught in the wild trees, the wild cow came up to the cave. And the cat followed and hid himself as before. And everything happened just as it did before. And the wild cow promised to give her milk to the woman every day in exchange for the wonderful grass. The cat went back through the wet, wild woods, waving his tail and walking his wild lone, just the same as before. But he never said a word to anyone. When the man and dog came home from hunting and asked the same question as before, the woman said, "Her name is not Wild Cow any more but Giver of Good Food. She will give us white milk for always and always and always. And I will take care of her when you and First Friend and First Servant go hunting.

Next day, the cat waited to see if any other wild thing would go up to the cave, but no one moved in the wet, wild woods. So the cat walked to the cave by himself. He saw the woman milking the cow and he saw the light of the fire in the cave and smelled the smell of the warm, white milk. The cat asked, "Where did the wild cow go?"

The woman laughed and said, "Wild thing out of the wild woods, go back to the woods again for I have braided up my hair and I have put away the magic blade bone, for we have no more need for friends or servants in our cave."

The cat said, " I am not a friend and I am not a servant. I am the cat who walks alone and I wish to come into the cave."

The woman said, "Why did you not come with First Friend on the first night? The cat grew very angry and said, "Has the wild dog been telling tales about me?"

The woman laughed and said, "You are the cat who walks alone. You are neither a friend nor a servant. You have said so yourself. Go off and walk by yourself."

Then the cat pretended to be sorry and said, "Must I never come into your cave? Must I never sit by the warm fire? Must I never drink the warm, white milk? You are very wise and very beautiful and you should not be cruel even to a cat."

The woman answered, "I always knew I was wise but I did not know that I was beautiful too. So I will make a bargain with you. If ever I say one word in your praise, you may come into the cave."

"And what happens if you say two words in my praise?"

"I never shall, but if I do, you may sit by the warm fire in the cave."

"And if you say three words in my praise?"

"I never shall, but if I do, you may drink the warm, white milk three times a day for always and always and always," said the woman.

Then the cat arched his back and said, "Now let the curtain at the mouth of the cave and the fire at the back of the cave and the milk pots that stand by the fire remember what you have said." And he went off through the wet, wild woods waving his tail and walking by himself.

That night the man and the dog and the horse came home from hunting. The woman did not tell them of the bargain she had made with the cat because she was afraid that they might not like it. The cat went far, far away, hiding himself in the wet, wild woods by his wild lone for a long time until the woman forgot all about him. Only the bat (the little upside down bat that hung in the mouth of the cave) knew where the cat hid, and every evening the bat would fly to the cat and tell him all that was happening in the cave.

One evening the bat said, "There is a baby in the cave. He is new and pink and fat and small and the woman is very fond of him."

The cat was listening closely and asked, "Ah yes, but what is the baby fond of?"

"He is fond of things that are soft and tickle. He is fond of warm things to hold in his arms when he goes to sleep. He is fond of being played with. He is fond of all these things," said the bat.

"Ah then," said the cat, "my time has surely come."

Next night the cat walked through the wet, wild woods and hid very near the cave until morning-time when the man and the dog and the horse went hunting. The woman was busy cooking that morning and the baby cried and interrupted. So she carried him outside the cave and gave him a handful of pebbles to play with. But still the baby cried. Then the cat came out of hiding and put out his paddy paw and patted the baby on the cheek, and it cooed and the cat rubbed against its fat knee and tickled it under its fat chin with his tail. The baby laughed and the woman heard him and smiled.

Then the bat (the little upside down bat that hung in the mouth of the cave) said, "A wild thing from the wild woods is playing most beautifully with your baby."

The woman straightened her back and cried out, "A blessing on that wild thing whoever he may be. I was a busy woman this morning and he has done me a service." That very minute and second the dried horse-skin curtain that was stretched at the mouth of the cave fell down — *Whoosh!* — because it remembered the bargain the woman had made with the cat. When the woman went to pick the curtain up — lo and behold — the cat was sitting comfortably inside the cave.

The cat said, "It is I, for you have spoken one word in my praise and now I can sit inside the cave for always and always and always. But still, I am the cat who walks alone."

The woman was very angry and clenched her teeth. She took up her spinning wheel and began to spin. But the baby cried because the cat had gone away and the woman could not hush it, for it struggled and kicked and grew black in the face.

The cat said, "Take a strand of the thread you are spinning and tie it to your spindle and drag it along the floor; and I will show you a magic that will make your baby laugh as loudly as he is crying now."

"I will do that because I am at my wit's end, but I will not thank you for it," said the woman."

She tied the thread to the little spindle and drew it along the floor. The cat ran after it and patted it with his paws and rolled head over heels and tossed it backwards over his shoulder and chased it between his hind legs and pretended to lose it and then pounced on it once more, until the baby laughed as loudly as he had been crying; and he scrambled and frolicked all over the cave until he grew tired and settled down to sleep with the cat in his arms.

The cat said, "Now, I will sing a song for the baby that will keep him asleep for an hour." He began to purr, loud and low, low and loud till the baby fell fast asleep.

The woman looked down at them and smiled. She said, "That was wonderfully done. Oh, cat! There is no doubt that you are very clever."

That very minute and second, the smoke of the fire at the back of the cave came down in clouds from the roof — *Puff, puff!* — because it remembered the bargain that the woman had made with the cat. When the smoke had cleared away — lo and behold — the cat was sitting cosily close to the fire. He said, "It is I, for you have spoken a second word in my praise and now I can sit by the warm fire at the back of the cave for always and always and always. But I am still the cat who walks alone.

Now the woman was very, very angry. She let down her hair, put more wood on the fire and brought out the broad blade bone of the shoulder of mutton and began to make a magic spell that would prevent her from saying a third word in praise of the cat. It was not a singing magic spell as she had done before; it was a still magic spell and by and by the cave grew so still that a wee, wee mouse crept out of a corner and ran across the floor.

The cat asked the woman, "Is that little mouse a part of your magic?"

"Oh, no indeed," said the woman, and she dropped the blade bone and jumped on the footstool in front of the fire, and she braided up her hair quickly for fear that the mouse might run up it.

The cat, ever watchful, said, "Then the mouse will do me no harm if I eat it?"

The woman answered, still braiding up her hair, "No, eat it quickly and I will be ever grateful to you."

The cat made one jump and caught the mouse and the woman cried, "A hundred thanks. Even First Friend is not quick enough to catch little mice as you have done. You must be very wise."

That very minute and second, the milk pot that stood by the fire cracked into two pieces — *Fffft!* — because it remembered the bargain she had made with the cat. And when the woman jumped down from the footstool — lo and behold — the cat was lapping up the warm, white milk that lay in one of the broken pieces.

The cat said, "It is I, for now you have spoken three words in my praise and now I can drink the warm, white milk three times a day for always and always and always. But still I am the cat who walks alone."

Then the woman laughed and gave the cat a bowl of the warm, white milk and said, "Oh, cat, you are as clever as a man, but remember the bargain was not made with man or dog and I do not know what they will do when they come home."

"What is that to me?" the cat replied. "If I have my place in the cave by the fire and my warm, white milk three times a day, I do not care what the man or the dog can do!"

That evening when man and the dog came into the cave, the woman told them the whole story of her bargain with the cat, while the cat sat by the fire and smiled. Then the man said, "Yes, but he has not made a bargain with me or with all proper men after me." Then he took off his two leather boots and he took out his little stone axe and he fetched a piece of wood and he laid them out in a row and said, "Now we will make our bargain. If you do not catch mice when you are in the cave for always and always and always, I will throw these things at you whenever I see you and so shall all proper men after me."

The woman was listening and said, "This is a very clever cat, but he is not as clever as my man."

The cat counted the things and they looked very knobbly. "I will catch mice when I am in the cave for always and always and always. But I am still the cat who walks alone and I will do as I please outside the cave."

"Not when I am near," said the man. "If you had not said that last bit, I would have put these things away. But now I will throw my two boots and my little stone axe at you whenever I meet you, and so shall all proper men after me."

The dog said, "Wait a minute. He has not made a bargain with me or with all proper dogs after me," and he showed his teeth and continued: "If you are not kind to the baby for always and always and always while I am in the cave, I will hunt you until I catch you and when I catch you I will bite you. And so shall all proper dogs after me.

"The woman, who was listening to all this, said, "This is a very clever cat but he is not as clever as the dog."

The cat counted the dog's teeth and they looked both numerous and very sharp. The cat answered, "I will be kind to the baby while I am in the cave for always and always and always, as long as he doesn't pull my tail too hard. But I am still the cat who walks alone and I will do as I please outside the cave."

"Not when I am near," said the dog. If you had not said these last words, I would have shut my mouth for always and always and always. But now I am going to hunt you up a tree whenever I meet you outside the cave, and so shall all proper dogs after me."

Then the man threw his two boots and his stone axe (that makes three things) at the cat and the cat ran out of the cave and the dog chased him up a tree.

And from that day to this, three proper men out of five will always throw things at a cat whenever they meet him, and all proper dogs will chase him up a tree. But the cat keeps his side of the bargain too. He will kill mice in the home and he will be kind to babies in the house as long as they do not pull his tail too hard. But, when the cat has done all this and when the moon rises and night falls, he is the cat who walks alone. Then he goes to the wet, wild woods or up the wet, wild trees or on the wet, wild roofs waving his wild tail and walking his wild lone.

Long-nose the Dwarf

Once upon a time there lived a cobbler — that is a man who makes and repairs shoes. This man did not earn much money with his work. He was poor. And so his wife earned extra money by growing vegetables in her little garden and selling them on the market. They had a little son called Jack and he used to help his mother. He sat by his mother's stall in the market and when people came past he shouted, " Fresh cabbages, carrots, peas, come and buy!" And people smiled at the little boy and they came and bought his mother's vegetables.

Now, one day a very strange-looking woman came to that market. Her face was thin and sharp and full of wrinkles, her eyes were red and her nose was big and pointed and hooked so that it nearly came down to her chin. She hobbled on a long stick and she hobbled right up to the stall where the cobbler's wife sat with her wee Jack and her baskets filled with fresh vegetables.

"Let me look at your greens!" said the old woman with a high shrill voice. And she bent over the baskets and clutched a cabbage with her long brown fingers, held it up to her nose and threw it back again. Then she picked up another and did the same; and she picked up another and did the same again. The cobbler's wife did not like that at all, for who would like to buy a cabbage that an old hag had held to her long nose? And little Jack did not like it either, how the old hag had treated their greens.

Jack said to her, "Don't put your nose into our things, for other customers won't like it!"

"Oh, you don't like my long nose then? Well, soon you will have a nose even longer than mine. Ha–ha–ha!"

But Jack's mother said, "Don't talk such nonsense to the child. If you want to buy anything, make haste and don't frighten my other customers away."

The old hag gave her a grim look. "Well and good, it shall be as you say. I will take these six cabbages but, as you see, I have to walk with a stick. I can't carry them. So let your little son carry the basket with cabbages to my house; it's not far from here."

Jack did not like to go with the old woman, but his mother ordered him to go, for she felt a little sorry for her. So the old woman paid, and Jack put the cabbages in a basket and followed her.

As she hobbled very slowly, it took quite a while until they came to a small tumbledown house. From the outside it looked a poor and rather dirty house, but when they went inside, little Jack was surprised to see that the walls of marble were decorated with gold and precious stones, and the floors were so smoothly polished that he slipped and fell. He was still more surprised when the old woman took a whistle from her pocket and blew on it, and several guinea pigs came running downstairs. They walked upright, like people, on two legs and were dressed like people too!

The old woman said to them, "Get my slippers, you lazy-bones, and quick!" The guinea pigs ran off and came back with the slippers and put them on her feet. These slippers were really coconut shells lined with silk. Once the old woman had them on, she could slide and glide with the shells on the polished floor, and it was a wonder to see.

Little Jack put the basket with the cabbages down and wanted to go back to his mother. But the old woman said, "Wait, I must reward you for carrying the cabbages for me. I am going to give you a nice plate of soup." And, in no time, the old woman cooked a pot of soup with all kinds of spices in it, and the smell was wonderful. The guinea pigs brought him a silver bowl of the soup with the marvellous smell, and Jack sat down and ate it with great enjoyment.

But as soon as he had finished the soup he felt terribly sleepy and drowsy, and although he said to himself, "I must go home, I must!" his eyes closed and he fell asleep. And it seemed to him that he had a strange dream: he dreamed that he was turned into a guinea pig, that he became a servant of the old woman, and he polished the shiny, smooth floors and then he worked in the kitchen and learned to cook the most marvellous dishes — especially pastries. In the end, he could make hundreds of pastries and he could cook wonderful soups that made your mouth water when you smelled them. It seemed to him in his dream that he was a guinea pig for seven years, serving the old woman.

But one day, after these seven years, the old woman went out while Jack was working in the kitchen. He had to look for some herbs and noticed a cupboard that he had not seen before. He opened it and saw a packet of herbs that were a strange bluish-green colour, and a flower that was as red as fire. This herb smelled just like the soup that he had eaten when he first came to the old woman. And when he smelled this herb he sneezed and woke up. He felt himself sitting in the armchair in which he had fallen asleep.

"What a strange dream that was," thought Jack, "but now I must go home." His limbs felt rather stiff from sleeping and he thought, "I must still be drowsy," for as he walked to the door, he was knocking his nose against cupboards and walls. The old woman's guinea pigs were running around him, but they did not stop him, and he walked out of the house and hurried to the market where his mother was.

As he walked in haste through the streets, he heard people saying, "Oh, look at that ugly little man with the long nose!" And he looked round to see if there was some little dwarf behind him, but all the people he saw looked quite ordinary.

At long last he came to the stall where his mother sat. She looked paler than usual and Jack rushed up to her, saying, "I'm sorry that I'm so late in coming back, Mother."

But she looked at him with horror and said, "You ugly dwarf. What do you want of me?"

"What do you mean, Mother?" said Jack in surprise.

"No more of your jokes, dwarf!" shouted the mother. "And don't you dare call me mother. I had a lovely little son who disappeared seven years ago and no one knows what happened to him. And I don't want to be called mother by a horrible creature like you. Go away!"

Poor Jack thought his mother must be ill, so that she didn't recognize him. And Jack, who could not understand what had happened, went off to his father the cobbler. He walked in and said, "Good day."

And the cobbler said to him, "Good day to you, little man." But he, too, did not recognize him.

Jack, who couldn't understand what had happened, said, "Tell me, master cobbler, have you not got a son to help you with your work?"

And the cobbler said, "Aye, I had a son, but he disappeared seven years ago and has not been heard of since. But what do you want here, little man — a new pair of shoes? Or perhaps a leather bag to put your nose in to keep it warm? It must be hard on you to have such a long nose in this bitter weather."

"A long nose?" said Jack in astonishment. " May I look in the mirror to see what's wrong with my nose?"

He went to the mirror and looked at himself, and when he saw what he looked like, tears came into his eyes. His nose had grown enormously, so that it hung over his mouth and chin. His body had become fat and round, so that it looked like a full sack, but his legs were like little thin stalks. He had not grown in these seven years at all: he was no taller than a little boy.

Now poor Jack knew it had not been a dream, that he had really been a servant of that old woman, and that she had made him so horrible-looking that even his own parents couldn't recognize him. They would never believe that their handsome little son had become a long-nosed, ugly dwarf. And so he sadly left the cobblers shop and wondered what he should do.

Then he remembered that he had learned to cook when he was with the old woman, that he could make all sorts of pastries and mouth-watering soups, and he thought that the king of his country might like a good cook, even if he were an ugly dwarf. Of course, he could not go to the king himself; the king already had a master cook, and Jack had to go to him and ask if he needed any help.

"Yes, I do need a helper," said the master cook, but not an ugly dwarf who knows nothing about cooking!"

"But I do!" cried Jack. "Please try me out."

"Well, the king wants for his lunch today: chicken soup with dumplings. Can you make it?" asked the master cook.

"I can make a better soup than he has ever had," said Jack. "Just give me all the herbs and spices I need for it."

So Jack set to work and made the soup, and the master cook was amazed at what a wonderful soup it was. And when the king tasted it, he called the master cook and said, "This is the loveliest plate of soup that I have ever tasted! Tell me, how did you make it?"

The master cook answered, " Well, Majesty, I didn't really make it myself, but this morning an ugly little dwarf with a horrible long nose came and asked to become my helper and I let him make the soup to try him out."

"He is a wonderful cook!" said the king. "And I want you to keep him to make all my soups for me."

And so Jack, the ugly dwarf with the long nose, became the special soup-cook for the king. He was well paid and people said of him, "He looks funny with his long nose, but the king likes him because he makes the best soups in the world."

And later Jack cooked other things for the king: roast lamb, chicken and goose. Jack always went to the market and shops himself to choose the most tender and plump chicken and geese for the king's dinner.

One day he went to the market and saw a woman he had never seen before, and she had a cage with three live geese in it. Jack thought the geese looked nice and plump so he bought them. But as he carried the cage with the three geese back to the king's palace, he was surprised to hear that two of them cackled as all geese do but the third sat silently in the cage and sighed and groaned like a human being.

Jack said aloud to himself, " I wonder if that goose is ill. I'd better kill and cook it first."

And, to his amazement, the goose said, " Let me live — I will bring you good fortune."

You can imagine how surprised Jack was about the speaking goose. When he had recovered from his astonishment, he said, "I would certainly not kill a goose that speaks human language! But I wonder if you really are a goose or if you have been changed into a goose by some magic power."

And the goose answered, "You are quite right; I am not really a goose. I'm the daughter of a great wizard, a magician. Unfortunately my father had a quarrel with a witch and she hated him so much that she changed me, his only daughter, and sold me to some peasants."

Jack said, " Poor you. You're even worse off than I am. I, too, have been changed into my present shape by a witch. She played a horrible trick on me by making me eat a plate of soup that smelled wonderfully."

"Oh," said the goose, "you too have fallen under the spell of a witch. But, you know, there must have been a magic herb in that soup, and if you knew what that magic herb was called, and where it could be found, the same herb would change you back into your real shape."

"I wish I knew that magic herb," said Jack, "but, alas, I don't know and so I have to remain a long-nosed dwarf. But I will certainly look after you and see that no harm will come to you."

And so Jack took the cage with the three geese to the king's palace. The other two geese were killed and eaten. For the goose who was really the daughter of a magician, Jack made a little wooden house and he fed her and looked after her. People wondered why the dwarf had a goose as a pet instead of a cat or a dog, but they didn't mind. If the funny little man liked the goose, well, other people like guinea pigs or white mice or hamsters, so why should he not have a goose? They didn't know, of course, that this was a special goose and that Jack had long talks with her in the evening when his work was finished.

Now, one day the king received a visitor, a proud prince from a foreign land, and Jack had to cook the most delicious food for this occasion. You see, the king was proud to have such a good cook and he wanted to show that no other king or prince had a better cook and ate better food than he. Whenever some delicious food was served the king would say, "Tell me, prince, can your own cook make this pastry nicer than my little dwarf?"

And the prince had to say, " No, your cook is much better than mine."

But, you know, the prince was very proud and conceited and he did not like to say at every meal, "Oh, yes, your cook is the better one." And so one day he said to the king, "You have a marvellous cook, but there is only one thing my cook at home can do better than yours: it's called 'wonder pastry'.

The king said, "I'm sure my dwarf can make that too," and he called Jack and said to him, "Listen, Long-nose, we want wonder pastry for dinner tomorrow, and if it's not on my table tomorrow your head will be cut off."

"Of course, of course you will have the wonder pastry tomorrow," said Jack. But he was trembling all over when he said it because he had never heard of that pastry and did not know how to make it!

In the evening he went to his friend the goose and told her his troubles. "Oh, don't worry," said the goose. "As it happens, I know how to make wonder pastry," and she told Jack exactly how to make it.

Well, Jack was happy again and the next day he used all his skill in cooking to make the wonder pastry, and he served it himself to the king and his visitor, the foreign prince.

The king said, "Mmmm! It's delicious, don't you think so, prince? Can your cook make it any better?"

And the prince answered, "Well, it's not bad, not bad at all. But, you know, something is missing — a special herb — and without that special herb the wonder pastry is not as delicious as my cook at home makes it."

"What?" shouted the king. "A herb is missing? You miserable dwarf. Why have you not put it in? I shall have your head cut off for this!"

Poor Jack was again trembling and he could only stammer, " I don't know what herb is missing ... what is that herb?"

And the foreign prince laughed and said, "Oh, it's a very rare herb; it's called 'sneeze-with-ease'. And without that herb sneeze-with-ease, the wonder pastry tastes only half as good as it should.

Then the king said, "I will spare your life for another day. Tomorrow you will make another pie made of wonder pastry, but this time with the herb sneeze-with-ease. And if I don't get it for dinner tomorrow, you will die."

And so Jack went again to his friend the goose to ask her where he might find the herb sneeze-with-ease. For, if he could not find it, his head would be cut off.

The goose said, "It's lucky for you that I'm the daughter of a magician, for my father has taught me to know all the herbs and so I also know the herb sneeze-with-ease. And tonight is the night of the full moon and it's just in the silvery light of the full moon that this herb blooms. But it grows only at the foot of chestnut trees."

"Are there any chestnut trees near the palace?"

"Oh, yes," said Jack, "about two hundred paces from the palace is a large grove of chestnut trees beside the lake."

"Well," said the goose, "then we must not waste any time but go there and look for the herb right away. Carry me on your arm and set me down once we are outside the palace, and I will help you to find the plant because I know what it looks like."

And so Jack took the goose on his arm and walked outside the palace, and people who saw him thought he was taking his pet for a walk. They came to the old chestnut trees by the lake and in the light of the full moon they both looked for the herb sneeze-with-ease. The goose walked under every tree and turned over every blade of grass but she could not find any sneeze-with-ease; and the poor goose became so desperate that she began to cry.

Just then Jack called out, "Look! On the other side of the lake there is one tree all by itself. Perhaps we shall find it there!"

The goose hopped and flew along and Jack, on his short legs, ran after her as fast as he could. And so they came to the tall, old chestnut tree. That tree cast a deep shadow; it was so dark that it was hardly possible to see what grew under it. Suddenly the goose stood still and flapped her wings with joy. She poked her head into the grass and pulled out something that she held out in her beak to Jack, and said. "This is the herb sneeze-with-ease and there's plenty of it growing here!"

Jack looked at the herb; it had leaves that were bluish green and the flower was a fiery red, and from the flower came a smell that he knew! Oh! That soup he had eaten in the old woman's house — it had smelled just like this! And Jack put his long nose into the flower and drew in the scent with all his might and it made him sneeze and sneeze and sneeze. And when he had finished sneezing, his head had come up from his shoulders, his legs were tall and strong, his body was slim, and his nose had shrunk and become a nice, small, straight nose. You can imagine his joy that he was no longer an ugly long-nosed dwarf.

And the goose cried out, "Oh, Jack, what a handsome young man you are now! No one would think that you were ever a long-nosed dwarf!"

And Jack said, "Yes, but it is you, dear goose, who have helped me, for without you I would never have known where to find the herb sneeze-with-ease. And as you have helped me, so I will help you. We shall not go back to the palace at all. I have finished cooking for the king. I shall take you back to your father and, as he is a great magician, he will most certainly be able to take the evil spell from you."

And so the same night they set out, and by noon the next day they came to the castle of the magician. The magician was very surprised when a handsome young man came in with a goose under his arm and said, "I have brought your daughter back to you."

The magician had not known what had happened to his daughter, but now he quickly spoke a powerful spell, and there stood, in place of the goose, a beautiful girl.

Of course, Jack married the wizard's daughter, and then he went to see his parents who, this time, did recognize him and cried tears of joy. Jack had brought them rich gifts from the magician so that they were no longer poor.

So they were all happy; that is, all except the king, who still wanted his wonder pie made with the herb sneeze-with-ease! The ugly little cook with the long nose had suddenly disappeared and no one knew where he had gone. There was no one to make delicious meals for him any more. There was no one to make a wonder pie for him, and his visitor, the foreign prince, went off and said, "You see, only my cook can make a wonder pie properly."

The Square Box

Once upon a time there lived a poor peasant who had an only son called Ivan. When Ivan was grown up he said to his father, "Our little farm is not big enough, dear father, to feed both of us. I will go out into the world and find work and earn my own living."

And so Ivan left his home and travelled far until he came to a big city. In that city he walked through the streets to see if anyone would need his help.

As he passed a big house a man looked out of the window and said, "Hey you, young fellow, I need a servant and you look strong. Would you like to work for me?"

"Yes," said Ivan, "I would."

And so the man said, "Mind you, you have to work ten years for me before you get your reward — and I won't tell you what it is."

"That's fine by me," said Ivan. "I will work ten years for you and I will be happy and satisfied with any reward you give me."

"You will not regret it," said the man, who was really a wizard — a magician — but Ivan did not know it.

And so for ten years Ivan worked for the man. He swept the floors, he laid the fire in the kitchen every morning, he worked in the big garden and carried messages for his master every day. In all this long time his master never paid him anything.

When the ten years were over, his master said to him, "Well, Ivan, you have served me well and here is your reward." And he gave Ivan a little square box and a little key.

Ivan said, "Thank you very much and goodbye." And he left his master.

Once he was out of the house he became very curious about what there might be in the square box, and so he took the little key and opened it. And what did he see? He saw the box was empty — there was nothing in it! Ivan was a bit annoyed but there was nothing he could do. He locked the square box again and put the key in his pocket and then he walked on, still wondering why he had been given such a poor reward for ten years' hard work.

He was already outside the city when his hand, in which he carried the box, started to get tired. He chucked it from one hand to the other and, as soon as he had done that, there stood before him twelve giants, and the tallest of the giants said, "We are your servants and we shall do anything you want us to do."

Ivan said, "Well then, build a castle here for me." And he had hardly spoken the words when a beautiful castle rose up before him. So Ivan became the king of this great, wonderful castle and he had many servants. He always kept his little square box on a table beside his throne.

One night a thief broke into the castle, and when he saw the square box on the table he wondered what great treasure might be in it. So the wicked thief took the square box and went off and nobody saw him.

Well, once the thief was outside the castle, he looked at the box and found that he could not open it — he had no key. He wondered if he should throw it away and, as he wondered what to do, he chucked it from one hand to another and there stood the twelve giants before him, and they said, "We are you servants; we shall do what you command."

And the thief said, "Well, I want to be king of this castle! Throw the other king out into a very deep pit!" And that is what the giants did. The thief became king of that castle and poor Ivan was thrown into a pit so deep that he could not climb out. What made it even worse was that people used this pit to throw dead animals into. When a sheep or a dog died people threw it into this pit. But they took no notice of Ivan.

Ivan was in despair; how could he ever get out? Just then he saw a great eagle swooping down and taking a dead sheep in its talons and flying away with it. Suddenly Ivan knew how to save himself. He took his leather belt and tied himself to another dead sheep that was lying in the pit, and when the eagle came a second time to take a sheep, it took Ivan away with it, because he was tied to the sheep. The eagle flew with its burden to a pine tree and there he perched on a branch. Ivan quickly untied his leather belt and climbed down the tree. He had got out of the deep pit, but what should he do now to get his castle back?

Ivan remembered that he still had the key to the magic square box in his pocket. Perhaps the key also had magic powers. So Ivan took the key and threw it from one hand to the other. And right away, one terribly tall giant stood before him and said, "I am your servant. I shall do what you command."

Ivan said, "First of all, bring me my square box from the castle." And one, two, three, the giant held out the square box to Ivan. As soon as he had the box again, he chucked it from one hand to the other and, as before, the twelve giants appeared. At Ivan's command the thief was thrown out and Ivan became again the true and rightful king of the castle and lived happily ever after.

Long-legs

Once upon a time there lived a peasant and his wife. Their little house stood near a forest. One day the peasant went into the forest and as he walked along a path, he came to a bramble bush. There was something moving and struggling in the branches and the peasant bent down to see what it was. It was a rabbit that had been caught in the prickly brambles; it tried to get out but it could not. The peasant took pity on the poor rabbit and he used his stick to lift the branches, so the rabbit could get free and run away.

Well, the next night the peasant had a dream, and in that dream there stood before him a large rabbit with a crown on its head. And the rabbit said, "Because you have been kind to one of my people you will be rewarded. You will have a child and this child will be able to run faster than anyone in the world." That was the peasant's dream and soon afterwards the peasant's wife had a baby: a boy!

As this baby boy grew up, his parents and all the other people who knew him were amazed because he had very long legs. When the boy was seven years old his legs were already as long as a grown-up's. And when the boy became grown-up, his legs were as long as a whole man. With his long legs he could run faster than anybody else, and all people called him "Long-legs".

One day the king of the country came with his men to hunt deer in the forest. Long-legs wanted to see the king. The king and his men were riding after one particular deer and trying to catch it, but this deer was much faster than the horses and so got farther and farther away from them. The king shouted, "The man who can catch that deer for me will be given a bag full of golden coins!"

Now, Long-legs was running along with the king's riders (which he could do quite easily!) and he heard what the king had said. He began to run much faster, and overtook the riders and the king. He left them behind, and he ran and ran until he caught up with the deer. He held it by its horns until the king arrived, then they took it to the king's garden where his daughter could play with it.

The king was very pleased with Long-legs and gave him the bag of gold coins. Then he said, "You know, I could use a fellow who can run so fast; will you come into my service?"

And Long-legs answered, "Yes, I will." And so he became one of the men who served the king.

Now, one day the king's daughter was walking in her garden when she saw a beautiful white horse. She wondered how this horse had got into her garden; was it, perhaps, a gift from her father? She went nearer to the horse — it seemed quite tame — and then she got onto its back. But as soon as she sat there, the horse began to run. It galloped to the wall of the garden, jumped over the wall, and it ran off with the king's daughter crying and crying.

But this horse wasn't a real horse; it was a wizard in disguise, who had changed himself into a horse so that he could get hold of the princess and take her away!

When the king heard what had happened to his daughter, he was very upset, and he cried, "Any man who brings my daughter back to me can marry her!"

And Long-legs said to himself, "Surely this is the time when I really have to run fast!" And he started to run, faster and faster and faster! He ran so fast that people who saw him coming past only saw a blur — something whizzing past And, as he was running so fast, Long-legs soon caught up with the white horse.

Now the white horse, too, put on speed and galloped with all its might. But, you know, no matter how fast the horse ran, Long-legs still came nearer and nearer. The white horse tried to run ever faster, so Long-legs, too, ran faster and faster. Then Long-legs caught up with the white horse and, as he came alongside while still running, he lifted the king's daughter from the horse's back. Just then, the white horse stumbled over a rock and fell and broke its neck. And that was the end of the wizard.

Long-legs took the princess home to her father the king. And they were married and lived happily ever after.

A Tale of Two Children

In the midst of a large forest there lived a witch. During the day she changed herself into a cat or an owl, but in the evening she took her proper shape: an evil-looking old woman with red eyes and a hooked nose that almost came down to her chin. She lived in a castle and anybody who came within a hundred paces of that castle had to stand still and could not move at all, and could not stir from the place until the old witch said, "You can go." If such a person was a boy, the witch would let him go, but if it was a girl, and especially a little girl, then she would change her into a bird and put her in a cage and keep her in a room in the castle.

The people who lived in the countryside around the forest always warned their children, "Don't ever go into that dark forest; many children have already disappeared and have never come back. So be careful; don't even go near it! And never go into it." Most children obeyed their parents; they played in the meadow, by the river and on the hills, and they kept well away from the dark wood. But not all children did so.

There were a little boy and his sister and one day they were playing in the fields. They saw a big black cat and they went to stroke it. But the cat seemed to be shy and he ran off, but only a few steps. Then it sat down and looked at them. So the little boy and the little girl ran after the cat, and as they came nearer the cat ran a few steps farther. The children thought it was fun to play tig with the cat so they kept on running after the animal, and they did not even notice that they were running into the dark wood. Suddenly they couldn't see the cat any longer, and they looked about. There were trees all around them and they didn't know which way to go; they were lost in the forest!

The little girl began to cry because she was afraid, but her brother, although only a little boy, said, "Don't cry, sister, and don't be afraid. I am with you and I will help you and protect you whatever happens. But we cannot stay where we are just now. We must search for a path which will take us out of this forest." He took his sister by the hand and they walked on.

As they walked on they saw something through the trees. What was it? They went a little nearer and then they saw it was the wall of a castle. And the little boy remembered that people spoke about a witch's castle in the forest, and he called out, "Oh, we mustn't go any nearer to that castle." But it was already too late!

The little sister beside him was already changed into a bird — before his very eyes — a nightingale which flapped its wings in fear, crying, "Jook, jook, jook!"

And around the nightingale there flew an owl that cried, "Toohoo, toohoo!" And the little boy could do nothing to help the nightingale. He couldn't move; he stood there like a stone. He couldn't speak and he couldn't weep and he couldn't move his hands or feet.

Soon after the sun set, and as soon as it was dark, the owl flew into a bush, and out of the bush came the evil-looking old woman. She caught the nightingale in her hand and took her away. The little boy was still standing there and could not move. But, after a little while, the old woman came back and mumbled a spell, and right away the boy was freed.

He fell on his knees before the old witch. "Please, please, give me back my little sister!"

But she only answered, "You will never see her again!" and walked away.

And the boy cried and cried but he could do nothing. After a time he found a way out of the forest, but he did not want to go back to his mother and father without his sister. He went to another village and became a shepherd boy. But he always thought about his sister and prayed to God to get his sister away from the witch.

After a long time, he had a dream. In his dream he saw a blood-red flower and in the middle of this flower there was a pearl. He dreamed he picked this flower, and with it he went to the witch's castle. And everything he touched was freed from enchantment. In the end he found his sister and she was changed from a bird back into a girl again.

The morning after the dream, he began to look for the blood-red flower. He went over hill and dale, he looked in rivers and searched forests. It took him nine days, but on the ninth day, in the morning, he found the blood-red flower and in the middle was a large dewdrop as big as the finest pearl.

Now that he had found the flower, he set out for the witch's castle in the middle of the dark, gloomy forest. At long last, after many days' journeying, he came again to the walls of the castle. He was one hundred paces from it, but he was not held stiff like a stone because the flower protected him, and he walked on. He came to the door of the castle and he touched it with the flower and the door sprang open. When he was in the castle he heard the singing and twittering of thousands of birds, and he followed the sound and came into a big hall where all the birds were in cages. The witch was there too, feeding the birds. But when she saw the boy, her face turned red with fury and she shouted at him. She wanted to scratch him with her long nails, but she couldn't get near him because he was protected by the blood-red flower. The boy took no notice of her, and he looked into all the cages for the nightingale which was his sister. Just then, he saw the witch creeping to the door with a cage in her hand, and in the cage was the nightingale!

The boy swiftly ran to the witch and touched her with the flower. She lost all her magic powers and could no longer bewitch anyone. Then he touched the cage and the cage door opened; the nightingale hopped out, looked up at him and called joyfully, "Jook, jook, jook!"

Then the boy touched the nightingale with the flower and there before him stood his sister; she cried with joy and kissed him. He went round all the other cages and touched them with the magic flower and they all became girls again. They were all very happy to be changed back into girls and they thanked him. And brother and sister went home to their parents. Their father and mother had already given up hope of ever seeing their children again, so you can imagine how delighted they were to see them.

And, as the witch no longer had any magic powers, it was no longer dangerous to go into the forest. From then on people walked in it and children played in it, and if anyone saw a cat or an owl they were no longer afraid of it.

King Grizzly Beard

A great king had a daughter who was very beautiful, but she was also proud and conceited. And when princes came and wanted to marry her, the proud princess thought that not one of them was good enough for her. She didn't just say to the prince, "No, I don't want to marry you." She teased them and made fun of them and she didn't care that this hurt the princes very much.

One day the king, her father, held a great feast and he invited many princes who wanted to marry his beautiful daughter. And at this feast, all the princes sat in one row and the princess walked along this row and she said something unkind and spiteful to each of the princes who sat there.

The first prince was rather stout and she said loudly, so that all could hear, "Look, he's like a barrel!" The next prince was very tall and she said to him, "Oh dear, he looks like a maypole." The next one was short and she said, "Isn't he like a dumpling?" The next prince was pale, and the naughty princess said, "Hello, Paper Face." And to the next, who had a red face, it was, "Hello, Poppy Face."

There also sat in the row a young king who was more than a prince, and he wore a beard. When she saw him, the naughty princess began to laugh and laugh, and she shouted, "Ho, look at him! His beard is like a grizzly old mop; he should be called Grizzly Beard!"

Now her father, the old king, was very annoyed that his daughter behaved so badly to all these noble guests, and he said to her in front of all the people in the hall, "You ill-behaved, rude girl! You don't deserve to be the wife of a prince or a king! I swear now that I will give you as wife to the first beggar who comes to the door!"

When all the guests went away, the naughty princess sat in her room crying because her father had promised her to a beggar man.

120

Two days later there came a man dressed in rags. He was so dirty that you could hardly see his face under the grime and dust on his skin. And this dirty fellow sang a little song at the door of the palace and begged people to give him a few pence.

The old king said, "Bring this beggar man to me." And the dirty-looking fellow came and sang his little song for the king.

The king said, "That was a very nice song. Do you know how I'm going to reward you for it?"

The beggar man answered, "Perhaps you will give me a gold coin?"

The old king said, "No, something much better."

And the beggar said again, "Perhaps, then, a bag of gold?"

"No," said the old king, "I shall give you my daughter as your wife."

The princess cried and wept and begged her father to forgive her naughtiness, but the old king said, "I have sworn to give you to the first beggar who came along and what I have sworn I must keep." And so the beggar and the princess went to church and were married.

Then the old king said to his daughter, "Now, get ready to go; you are now the wife of a beggar and you must travel with your husband wherever he goes."

And so the beautiful princess, who was used only to the finest silk dresses and to the most delicious food and to soft beds to sleep in, had to be dressed in the coarsest cloth and had to eat only what others had left, and she had to sleep on the kitchen floor or out in the open beside her husband. And she was very, very unhappy.

One day she and her beggar husband came to a large forest and the princess said to him, "Tell me, who owns this beautiful forest?"

The beggar answered, "It belongs to King Grizzly Beard, and if you had married him it would have belonged to you too."

The princess sighed and said, "Oh, how foolish I was. I wish I had married King Grizzly Beard!"

As they walked on, they came to great meadows that were lovely to see, with their fresh green grass and scattered over with daisies and buttercups. The princess asked again, "Who owns these fine meadows?"

The beggar, her husband, said, "King Grizzly Beard owns them, and if you had married him, these meadows would be yours too."

And again the princess said, "I was indeed foolish not to marry King Grizzly Beard!"

As they walked on they came to a great city with beautiful buildings. The princess asked, "Who does this fine city belong to?"

And her husband, the beggar, answered, "It is all King Grizzly Beard's, and if you had married him all this would be yours too!"

And the princess said, "How I wish I had married King Grizzly Beard; how foolish I was!"

"Well, you have married me and I am good enough for you," said the beggar.

At last they came to an old, little hut and the princess said, "I wonder who this ramshackle old thing belongs to?"

And her husband, the beggar, answered, "It belongs to me and it is our home where you and I are going to live."

The princess cried out, "Where are your servants?"

And the beggar answered, "Poor people like us have no servants, and what we want to be done, we do ourselves. So now we're going to make a fire and put on water and cook our supper because I'm hungry and tired."

Now, the princess had never made a fire or cooked anything in her life and she didn't know what to do. In the end, the beggar had to help her and do most of the work.

The next morning the beggar woke the princess very early and said, "Get up and clean the house!"

The princess got up, but she had never handled a broom in her life and she was so clumsy with it that the beggar had to help her again. He grumbled a lot and said, "You're not much use as a housewife." And the next day he said, "There's no more food in the house and there's no money to buy food. You must make something that you can sell to earn money. I will bring you branches from a willow tree, and you must weave them into baskets that I can sell in the market." He went out and brought back long, slender, willow branches and gave them to the princess.

Well, she tried to weave them to make baskets, but the tender skin on her hands was not used to such work and became sore and bled. She started to cry and could not go on with her work.

The beggar said, "I can see you're not much use at making baskets. Perhaps you'll be better at spinning." And so he gathered wool from the hills, but the threads cut her fingers until blood came and she cried with pain and had to stop.

The beggar said, "I've never seen such a useless wife! But we'll try something else. I have a lot of pots and pans that I can take to market, and you will stand there and sell them while I do other work."

The princess said, "Oh no. If people from my father's court come and see me selling pots and pans, they will laugh at me!"

And the beggar said, "I don't care if they laugh or not. You must do some work or you'll have no food." So the princess had to stand in the market selling pots and pans. And people liked to buy from the beautiful woman, so at first she did well. But later a drunken soldier rode his horse right through her pile of earthenware pots and pans, and they were all broken to pieces.

She came crying back home to her husband, the beggar, and he grumbled, "You were silly to put the pots in a place were horses were passing. You are no good even for this kind of work. You can't cook, you can't weave baskets or spin wool and now, it seems, that you cannot be trusted with a few pots and pans! But I have found other work for you. I have been to the king's palace and have asked if, by any chance, they need a kitchen maid, and they need one and they will take you!"

And so the princess went the next day to the palace and became a kitchen maid. She had to help the cook who gave her all the work that she did not like herself: peeling potatoes, washing vegetables, making the fires, taking out the ashes and, of course, the washing up! It was hard work for hours and hours every day, but at least she was given food for her beggar husband and herself.

Then one day, while she was working in the kitchen, she heard people saying, "The king is going to get married! Look! All the lords and ladies of the court are invited." The princess went to the window and looked out and there were all the courtiers in their splendid clothes! And the princess felt terribly sad, and she was sorry that she had been so proud and rude and so had deserved her punishment.

When the day's work was over, the cook gave her some scraps of meat to take home. She put them in her basket and covered them carefully with a cloth so that people in the streets wouldn't see that she was carrying bits left over from other people's meals. But just as she was going out of the kitchen, the king himself came in. He was dressed in beautiful cloth of gold, and when the princess looked at him she saw that he was King Grizzly Beard. She wanted to run away from him but he said to her, "Oh, kitchen maid, I want you to come and be my partner at the dance."

Of course, she did not want to go, but the king took her by the hand and pulled her away, so she had to come along in her dirty working clothes and with the basket on her arm.

When she came amongst the lords and ladies, all in their beautiful clothes, she felt so ashamed that she again tried to run away. But King Grizzly Beard held on to her hand, and in the struggle the cover came off her basket and the bits of leftover meat fell out. The lords and ladies laughed and jeered at her.

At this, the poor princess began to weep with shame. She pulled her hands free and hurried towards the door. But King Grizzly Beard was faster. He got to the door before her and said, "Wait, look at me. Don't you recognize me? I was disguised as the beggar man who lived with you in the hut. I was also the soldier who rode his horse into your pots and pans and I have done all this because I love you; but I wanted to cure you of your pride and punish you for the rude and unkind things you said about me and many others. But now all that is over. I am sure you have learned some wisdom now. You will never be proud and spiteful again, will you? And so it is time that we had a proper royal wedding feast."

Then the servants brought her the most beautiful robes, and her own father came with his whole court, and the wedding feast was the most wonderful that you can imagine! And no one was happier than the princess, and she never forgot the hard lessons that she had learned.

Hans in Luck

Do you think that a greedy person can be happy? No, they can never be happy, because whenever they get what they want, they just want more and more. So they will never be content with what they have. But if you are not greedy, if you are content with what you have, you will be happy whether or not you have a little or a lot. I am going to tell you a story of such a person, a young man called Hans, who was content with whatever he had.

This young man Hans had worked for a master for seven years and he had worked hard and well. At the end of the seven years the master said, "I am very pleased with the work you have done, Hans, and as it is time for you to go home to your parents I shall give you the reward you deserve." And the master gave Hans a lump of pure gold, a lump as big as his head!

Hans was very pleased with this reward. He took out his big handkerchief, wrapped the lump of gold in it, put it on his shoulder and set off home.

He walked on and on and the sun was shining and it got very hot. Hans was sweating with the heavy burden of gold on his shoulder. Just then, a man came riding past on a horse and said, "What are you carrying on your back?"

"A lump of gold," said Hans.

And the horseman said, "That lump of gold is not much use to you, is it? It weighs down on you; you have to carry it. I'm much better off on my horse because the horse carries me and I'm sitting comfortably on it."

"Yes, quite true. You are more comfortable on your horse than I am with my lump of gold."

The horseman thought for a moment then said, "I am kind hearted and quite willing to swap with you. Give me your lump of gold and I will give you my horse."

Hans answered, "Will you really? All right then, you can have the gold for the horse."

So the horseman got off his horse and walked away with the lump of gold, and Hans climbed on to the horse and rode off. He was delighted that his legs could rest and that the horse carried him. But the horse was walking slowly and Hans wished it would go faster. So he clicked his tongue and it worked: the horse started to trot, then run, then gallop. But Hans was not used to riding on a galloping horse and soon he fell off. He fell into a ditch and, as he picked himself up, a peasant who was passing stopped the horse from running away.

The peasant was leading a cow and he said to Hans, "A horse isn't much use to you, my lad. You are lucky you haven't broken any bones! You would be much better off with a cow like mine. You can milk it and from the milk you can make butter and cheese. These are things you can eat, and they're much better than a horse that throws you into a ditch."

Hans said, "You're right. A cow would be more useful!"

"Well," said the peasant, "as you're a nice boy, I shall do you a favour: you give me your horse and I shall give you my cow." And Hans agreed. He took the cow for the horse and went off happily.

As he drove the cow before him he became very thirsty as it was a hot day, and Hans thought to himself, "Well, I've got a cow; I will milk her and have a nice drink!" He tied the cow to a tree and held his leather cap under it and started to milk her. But you all know that milking is a special art and Hans did not know this art — and so no milk came. But something else happened: the cow kicked Hans on the head and he fell to the ground and nearly fainted!

Just then a butcher came along with a wheelbarrow, and in the wheelbarrow sat a pig. The butcher helped Hans to get up.

"My poor lad, it's no use trying to milk this cow; she's too old for that, although she can still be used for meat. If you like, I will give you my little pig in exchange for her. You can take the pig home and feed it for a while, then kill it and get some bacon and ham from it."

Hans said, "Oh yes, that sounds fine! Yes, you take the cow and I'll take the little pig!" And so Hans went along with the pig on a string behind him and he was happy, thinking how nice the bacon would be for his breakfast. But he did not bring the pig home, because something else happened.

Hans was walking along with his little pig on a string, and he thought to himself how lucky he was that everything had turned out so well for him: when the lump of gold became a heavy burden he could change it for a horse; when the horse had thrown him he had changed it for a cow; when the cow had kicked him he had changed her for a little pig; it had all turned out fine for him. And just as he was walking along, he met another young man and this young man was carrying a goose under his arm.

The young man said, "How did you get hold of that pig, young friend?"

And Hans answered, "Oh, a man gave it to me for a cow I had."

And the young man with the goose said, "I'm afraid you're in trouble; this pig was stolen from a village nearby, and if the people who own the pig see you with it, they will think you're the thief. And they will beat you and put you in prison."

"Good heavens!" said Hans. "What am I to do?"

The young man with the goose said, "Well, I know my way around here and I know where I could hide that pig. I will take the pig and you can have the goose for it. It will give you an egg for every breakfast and at Christmas it will make an nice meal."

Hans answered, "Oh, thank you very much. I am really lucky to have met you." So the young man went off with the pig and Hans continued his journey with the goose. Hans thought, "I'm very lucky to have this goose; there will be eggs, there will be roast meat and lots of fat to use for all sorts of things; there will be soft feathers to put into my pillow. Oh, yes indeed, I am lucky!"

He walked on until he came to a village, and in the village he met a man who sharpened knives and scissors. He had a big stone wheel and he turned the stone wheel with his foot and held the edge of the knife against the wheel to sharpen it. While the man was sharpening one knife after another, he was singing merrily. Hans watched the man for a little while and then he said, "You seem to enjoy your work!"

"Indeed I do," he answered. "People pay me well for making their old knives and scissors sharp again. I always have plenty of money in my pocket and all I have to do is turn a wheel. Wouldn't you like to own such a wheel that turns so easily?"

And Hans said, "Yes, yes, I would."

The man said, "Well, I have another wheel just like this one and I will exchange it for the goose you are carrying."

Hans said, "That is most kind of you; yes, please. You take the goose and I will take the wheel and earn money with it when I get home." And so Hans gave the man his goose and took the heavy, stone sharpening-wheel.

So Hans walked on, but, you know, the stone wheel was much heavier than the lump of gold he had carried to begin with and Hans became tired and thirsty. Just then he saw a well. He went to it and put his heavy stone on the edge of the well. As he bent down to get water, he pushed against the stone by mistake and it tumbled down into the well with a great splash, and sank right to the bottom. Hans laughed with joy because now he was rid of the heavy stone, and he thanked God that he did not have to carry it any farther.

He said to himself, "I am very lucky indeed that I can now go back to my mother without having to carry anything, without having a horse that throws me, a cow that kicks me, a pig that was stolen, or a goose that I have to carry under my arm. Oh, I am very lucky." And he ran and ran joyfully until he was home again with his mother. She was so glad to see him and to have him home again that it didn't matter at all that he had brought nothing back. You see, if people are not greedy, they can be perfectly happy just like Hans, even although he had nothing.

The Harp with Five Strings

There are all kinds of instruments with which to make music: the piano, the violin, the flute. Can you tell me any others? But there is also an instrument that you don't hear or see very often these days, but which people used to play a lot in the olden days — it's called a harp. A harp has strings and you pluck them with your fingers. I am going to tell you a story of such a harp. This harp had five strings, one for each finger of the hand.

Once upon a time there was a king who owned a harp with five strings. This was a harp with magic powers. When the king's soldiers had to go and fight against enemies, the king would take his harp and play a tune on it. And the soldiers heard the tune and they felt strong and brave and they went out and fought so bravely that the enemy was soon driven away. And when the battle was over and the soldiers came back tired from the fighting and with sore wounds, the king would again play the harp with five strings. But he played a different tune, and when the tired and sore soldiers heard this they felt fresh and their wounds and cuts did not hurt them any more. It was a wonderful harp! So every time enemies came to fight the king who had the magic harp, they were driven away and lost their battles.

The enemies thought and thought about how they might get hold of the harp with five strings. And what they did was this: they came again and fought against the king and his soldiers. But while the king and his men were in battle fighting, some of the enemies ran quickly to the king's palace and stole the wonderful, magic harp. When the king and his men came back they saw that the harp with the five strings had gone! But the king realized that only the enemies could have taken the harp and so he quickly went after them.

As he came to the enemies' castle, he heard their shouting and singing from afar; they were feasting because they had taken the harp.

The king walked into the castle and came into a big hall, and there were men and women eating and drinking and singing — and his magic harp was hanging on the wall.

The men in the hall saw the king and they drew their swords to kill him. But, before they could do anything, the king called out to his harp, "Come to me, my harp!" and the harp with five strings knew his voice, and it leaped from the wall and it flew through the air and came to rest in his hands. As soon as the harp was in his hands, the king plucked the strings and he played a tune that was called "The Music of Tears." When the men, who had their swords ready drawn to kill the king, heard the music of tears, they could do nothing but cry and sob and weep.

The king made them weep for a time, and then he played another tune called "The Music of Laughter" and as soon as they heard it, all the people in the hall burst out laughing. And they laughed and slapped their sides and they could not stop. The swords fell from their hands and they simply fell to the floor.

Then, once more, the king plucked the strings of his harp for another tune, called "The Music of Sleep." And when he played that tune, all the people in the hall could not keep their eyes open; the soft music made them sleepy and soon they were all sound asleep.

And when they were all in a deep slumber, the king went away with his magic harp of five strings and no one ever tried to steal it again.

The Story of Ten Fingers

Once upon a time there was a boy who was clumsy with his hands. When he took a glass to drink water, the glass was certain to slip from his fingers and break into pieces. His mother would not let him help her with the washing-up, because every time he helped her a few plates were broken. When he ate his soup, at least once a week he upset his plate and the soup was all over the tablecloth. He could not tie his shoelaces and he could not untie them; his fingers were far too clumsy! And his mother used to say sometimes, "My poor boy; it seems you have ten little sticks and not ten nimble fingers like other people!"

The boy was very sad that he was so clumsy, and he would have liked to have nimble fingers that could do things well and that wouldn't let things slip and break. But, there it was: his fingers just could not do anything well or useful.

One day, when he had again broken something (a beautiful flower vase), he went into a nearby forest all by himself and was very unhappy. Then, suddenly, he stood still and looked about him with wonder for he saw ten little men, dwarfs, in a glade. And it was quite wonderful what these little men did! One of them took the fine threads of a spider's web, and one, two, three! He had woven them into the finest silk. Another little dwarf took dewdrops and they glittered in the sun like diamonds. Yet another caught sunrays and twisted them into fine threads of gold, and he put these into rocks. Another dwarf had a fine brush and paint. Birds came to him and he painted their feathers so that they gleamed in the sunlight. So every one of the ten dwarfs did something that could only be done with great skill.

When the boy saw how clever the dwarfs were with their hands, he gave a deep sigh. At the sound of his sigh the dwarfs turned round and saw him. One of them said, "Why are you sad and sighing, my boy? Don't you like what we are doing?"

"Oh, yes, I like it," said the boy, "but I only wish that I could do things as you do them, so quickly and so well. But I'm afraid that my fingers are no good at anything!"

And the dwarf said, "Well, perhaps we can help you. Hold out your hands." The boy held out his hands. Each dwarf whispered something to each finger.

The oldest of the dwarfs said, "Now each of your fingers — the two thumbs, the two forefingers, the two middle fingers, the two ring fingers and the two pinkies — know a secret that we have told them. And now that they know the secret, they will be clever fingers and not silly, clumsy fingers any more. All of sudden the ten dwarfs disappeared.

Well, the boy looked at his hands, at his fingers; they didn't look any different! But he wanted to try them out, so he ran home and there he saw his mother's knitting lying on the table. Before he had met the dwarfs he wouldn't have dreamed of trying to knit, but now he did, and his fingers worked deftly and skilfully and quickly. When his mother came in, she could not believe her eyes; and he had done such a lot!

From that day onwards, the boy could do anything he wanted with his hands and it always turned out well. More than that, he never broke anything again. But he could never do the wonderful things the dwarfs had done; his fingers were still human fingers and not the fingers of the little folk!

The Twelve Months

Twelve is a wonderful number. The first thing we learn about twelve is that a year has twelve months: January, February etc. Can you tell me the name of the month we are now in? The story I'm going to tell you is about the twelve months of the year.

Once upon a time there was a little girl called Mary. She was an unhappy girl because she lived alone with a nasty stepmother who did not like Mary at all. The poor girl had to work hard: scrubbing floors, cooking, washing clothes, sewing and working in the garden. And all the time her stepmother was after her, scolding her, nagging her and telling her that she was lazy and clumsy and was not working hard enough. Mary was never given enough to eat, she had to sleep on the floor in a corner of the kitchen and the wicked stepmother often beat her with a stick. It was a terrible life for poor Mary.

Now, there came a day, deep in winter, when the month was called January and, you know, people call January the ice month because it often brings ice and snow. That January was especially cold. All the rivers and lochs were frozen over and the roads were so deep under snow that you could not even see them. And a cold wind was blowing too.

During this especially cold weather, the wicked stepmother said, "Mary, I want some violets. Go into the forest and get me some."

Well, you know as well as I that violets are little blue flowers that grow only in spring, when it's warmer.

And so Mary said, "How can I find violets at this time of year, in January? There aren't any now."

But the stepmother shouted, "You horrible child! You do as you are told. Out you go and don't come back until you've found some violets, or I shall beat you with my stick." The stepmother took Mary by the arm and pushed her out of the door and closed and locked it after her.

So there was Mary, in a thin dress without a coat, and she shivered in the cold. But there was nothing she could do. She had to go, knee-deep through the snow, deep into the wood.

Mary walked and walked. She was nearly frozen with cold. She was so tired, she could hardly lift her feet. She was hungry, and she had, of course, not seen any flowers at all, and certainly no violets. In her unhappiness she prayed to God to help her.

After she had prayed she saw, far away, a light. As she walked towards the light she saw that it came from the top of a mountain. When she reached the top of the mountain she saw that there was a great fire. Around the fire were twelve stones and on the twelve stones sat twelve men: three men were old with long, white beards; three men were younger and had brown beards; and three men were still younger and they had no beards. And then there were another three, and they were so young that they were really just big boys. These twelve men were the months of the year.

The man who sat on the highest stone was called January, the ice month, and, of course, he was one of the old men with a long white beard. In his hand he held a long rod. Mary was afraid of these twelve men at first; she didn't know who they were and didn't dare to go nearer. But the fire seemed so warm, and remember, she was terribly cold. So she took courage, went up to the twelve men and said, "Please can I sit by the fire? I am shivering all over with cold."

January, the very old man, nodded and said, "What are you doing here, little girl? Are you looking for something?"

And Mary answered, "Yes, I'm looking for violets."

January said, "When I am ruling the world, when ice and snow cover the earth, that is no time to look for violets!"

"Oh, I know," said Mary sadly, "but my stepmother has told me that unless I come back with violets from the forest, she will take her stick and beat me. Please can you help me and tell me where to find violets?"

And January, the ice month, got up and went to a younger brother, saying, "Brother March, take my rod and sit on the highest stone." March went and sat down on the highest stone and he started to move his rod over the fire. Right away the flames burned higher and the snow around started to melt. The trees around grew little buds. The grass began to shoot, and among the grass appeared some flowers. And under a bush Mary saw some violets, as many as if she had spread out a blue handkerchief.

March said to Mary, "Quick, pick as many violets as you want."

Mary picked a big bunch and then she thanked the twelve months and hurried home to her stepmother.

The wicked stepmother had thought that Mary would die of cold out there in the snow. So she was very surprised when Mary came home with a big bunch of violets.

"Where did you find them?" asked the stepmother.

"Oh, on top of the mountain there were plenty of them," answered Mary.

Well now, the stepmother did not show her surprise but took the violets and put them in a little vase. The smell was lovely!

But the next day the stepmother thought of something else to drive Mary out into the snow and cold. She said to Mary, "Go out into the forest and find some strawberries for me."

"Goodness," said Mary, "how can there be strawberries when everything is covered with snow?"

But the stepmother shouted, "You naughty girl, always talking back! Out you go and don't dare come back without strawberries!" And she pushed Mary outside and locked the door behind her.

Mary cried and cried; how could she possibly find strawberries in January, the ice month? But she walked into the forest knee-deep in snow, she looked and looked and she walked and walked, and she shivered with cold and was terribly hungry. And then, again, she saw the fire on the mountain and she hurried towards it.

There round the fire sat the twelve men again: three handsome young boys, three young men, three with brown beards and three with white beards. And on the highest stone, as before, sat January, the ice month.

Mary said, "Please may I warm myself by your fire? I am shivering with cold."

And January said, "Yes, of course, but why have you come here again? Are you looking for something?"

Mary answered, "Yes, I'm looking for strawberries."

"This is no time to look for strawberries, when I rule the world with snow and ice," said January.

And Mary said, "I know, but my stepmother told me to bring strawberries, and if I come back without them, she will beat me. Please tell me where I can find strawberries?"

So January got up and went over to another brother who sat opposite him and said, " Brother June, sit on the highest stone and take my rod in your hand." And the beautiful month of June sat on the highest stone and moved the rod back and forth over the fire. And the flames of the fire rose up, higher and higher. The snow all around melted, grass grew high, the trees were full of leaves, birds sang and twittered and everywhere beautiful flowers grew. It was summer! There were flowers that looked like little white stars, but these white stars soon changed into strawberries. First they were green and slowly they became red and ripe.

The beautiful month of June said, "Quick, Mary, pick your strawberries."

And Mary picked and picked strawberries until her apron was so full that it could not hold any more! Then she said, "Thank you very much," and hurried home.

The wicked stepmother had hoped that Mary would die of cold in the forest, and she was very surprised when she saw her with an apron full of ripe strawberries. She only said in an unfriendly voice, "Where did you get these?"

And Mary answered as before: "Oh, on top of the mountain there were more than I could gather!"

The stepmother took all the strawberries, put sugar and cream on them and gobbled them all up by herself.

The next day she wanted Mary to get some rosy apples from the forest. Mary said, "This is no time of year to find apples on trees! The branches are bare; there aren't any leaves!"

The stepmother said again, "You naughty child; don't dare answer me back when I ask you to do something! Out you go and don't come back without apples or I will beat you with my stick!" And again she pushed Mary outside and locked the door behind her.

Mary walked knee-deep through the snow, shivering and hungry and she cried. Again she saw the fire on top of the mountain and she hurried towards it. At the fire, she saw again the twelve months of the year, each sitting on his own stone.

Mary begged again, "Please let me sit by your fire because I am so terribly cold!"

January said, "Why are you here again? What are you looking for this time?"

And Mary had to say, "Apples."

"You know very well that when I rule the world with ice and snow, there cannot possibly be apples growing on trees at the same time," said January.

And Mary answered, "But my stepmother wants apples. And if I go home without any, she will beat me."

Then January stood up and went to another brother, who had a short brown beard, and he said to him, "Brother September. Take the rod and sit on the highest stone." So September took his place on the highest stone and moved the rod over the fire. This time the fire did not flare up but simply glowed red, and the snow around melted. The trees were dropping their leaves and the wind carried them through the air. There were all kinds of flowers in bloom: nasturtiums, asters and Michaelmas daisies. Mary looked around, and there she saw an apple tree laden with rosy apples.

September said to her, "Quick, Mary, shake the tree." Mary shook the tree and one red apple fell down. She shook again and another fell.

Then September said, "Quick, take these two apples and go home, little Mary." So, Mary took the two little red apples and hurried home.

Mary arrived home and gave the two apples to her stepmother, who said, "Where did you find these?"

"Up on the mountain," said Mary. "There are plenty more on the tree."

And the stepmother said, "Then why have you brought back only two? Perhaps you have eaten all the others, you naughty girl!"

"Oh no, I haven't eaten any. I shook the tree twice and each time only one apple fell down. I was not allowed to shake the tree more than two times." And so the stepmother took the two apples and ate them, and they were so delicious she thought she had never eaten apples as tasty as these.

Then she said, "I'm going up the mountain myself to get more of these wonderful apples, and I will take as many as I like and shake the tree as often as I like, whether I get permission or not!" So the wicked stepmother put on a thick fur coat and walked out whilst Mary stayed at home.

The stepmother walked and walked in the deep snow but nowhere could she see an apple tree with apples on it! At long last she saw a light in the distance and she moved towards it. She saw that it came from a fire on a mountain and, as she walked to the top, she said to herself, "Ah! Now I have found the mountain where Mary found violets, strawberries and apples in deep winter." She came to the top of the mountain, and there she saw the great fire, the twelve stones and the twelve men sitting on the stones. The oldest man, January, was still sitting on the highest stone. The stepmother went straight to the fire to warm herself, without saying a word to the twelve men.

January asked her, "What are you doing here and what do you want?"

She answered, "That's none of your business, you old fool; I go where I like and I do what I like." When she had said this, she turned around and began to look for the tree with the lovely red apples.

But January was very cross because she had been so rude to him. He took his rod and moved it over the fire, and as soon as he did this the flames went down, an ice-cold wind began to blow, the sky became black with clouds and snow began to fall, thicker and thicker. There were so many snowflakes falling that the stepmother could no longer see where she was going. She walked and walked. On she went and on and the snowflakes kept falling. She walked and walked, and now she could no longer find her way out of the forest! She became very tired and cold, and in the end she fell down in the snow and she could not get up again. And that is where she died.

In the meantime, Mary was at home and had cooked the dinner and swept the house clean. She waited for her stepmother to come home again but, as you know, she could not come back.

When night came, Mary looked out of the window and saw the glittering stars, and the earth was white with freshly fallen snow. Mary wondered what had happened to her stepmother. The next morning she was still not back, and Mary thought she must have died in the snow and she said a little prayer for her.

Now Mary owned the house and its garden and she lived there very happily. She never forgot the kind men who were the twelve months of the year.

The Five Goats

There was once a boy who had to look after his father's five goats every day. He looked after them very well. Every morning he took them to the meadow. There was nice grass to eat and clear water to drink. Every evening he brought them home again, and they were milked and gave their creamy milk and shared it with people.

One evening the goats wanted to stay in the meadow. The boy could not get them into the stables. "Home, home, home you go! You have to be milked!" he cried. But the goats did not go and continued eating the juicy grass.

Then his sister came and said, "Wait, let me try. I will bring them inside." And she ran after the goats. But they still didn't want to go inside.

Just then, a dog came walking by. "Wait!" he cried. "I will bring them to the stables. My voice is much louder than yours. It will scare the goats and then I will bring them inside. *Woof, woof, woof!*" The dog ran behind the goats, but they did not get scared and ate from the juicy grass and did not go inside.

Then came the red fox to see why the dog was barking so loudly. "Let me try," said the fox. "The dog howls much too loudly. I know something better. I will soon get it done." The fox ran behind the goats and cried, "Hee, hee, inside you goats!" But the goats didn't take any notice and just continued eating from the juicy grass.

Then came the horse. "Let me fix this," he said. "I'm bigger than the fox. I can do more than a dog, and I have more legs than the boy." The horse ran to the goats and called, "It's nearly dark, goats. It's time for you to go to the stables." But the goats scarcely looked at the horse and continued to eat the nice fresh grass and did not go inside.

A bee came buzzing past. "What's happening here?" he asked. "Why are you still in the field so late?"

"The goats don't want to go inside," said the boy and the girl. "Nobody can get them into the stable: not the horse, nor the fox, nor the dog and nor can we."

"Yes, that's right," called the horse and the fox and the dog.

"Then it's my turn," said the bee. "I will lead them inside; let me show you how."

"You are much too small," said the children.

"You cannot make enough noise," said the dog.

"You cannot run on four legs around the field," said the horse.

"We'll see," said the bee and flew away. He flew straight to the biggest goat and buzzed, "*Bzzz, bzzz, zoom, zoom, zoom!*" in his ear.

The goat raised his head at this commotion in his ear and saw the bee. "What is this?" cried the goat. "I can't stand this terrible noise." And he took to his heels in the direction of the stable.

The second goat said, "If you're going home, so am I!" and started off.

The other goats called to her, "Let's all go together to the stable," and off they went.

And so the tiny bee managed to do what all the others had tried to do but failed.

A Tale of Nine Children

Once upon a time there was a peasant. He had a daughter who was so beautiful that all the people who saw her said that she was the most beautiful girl they had ever seen.

One day, three men came riding to this peasant's hut, and as they came in each one said, "I want to marry your daughter."

The peasant answered, "But, my dear gentlemen, I have only one daughter."

At this, all three shouted, "Tomorrow I shall come back for your daughter, and if you don't give her to me, I'll kill you!" And then they rode away.

Of course, the poor peasant was quite in despair! What should he do? If he gave his daughter to one of them the other two would kill him! He was so worried that he couldn't work and he decided to go for a walk.

He went to an old man who lived all by himself in a large wood, and people said he had strange powers. The peasant told this old man about his worries, and the old man said, "I will help you. Do you see this pig in my yard? And do you see that horse standing beside it? Take them both with you and let them sleep tonight in the same room as your daughter."

And the peasant did as he was told. He took the pig and the horse home and, at night, he put them both in the room where his daughter slept. And when he came in next morning, there were three girls in the bedroom, and they all looked exactly alike. Even the father couldn't tell which was his real daughter and which was the pig or the horse!

When the first man arrived, he gave him one girl, and the man rode away with his bride. Then came the second man, and he too was given a girl and rode away with her. The third man got the last girl and he also rode off with her. The peasant still didn't know which man had his real daughter.

And so, many years passed. The peasant wondered how his real daughter was and if she had any children who would be his grandchildren. He decided to search for her.

He came to a house, and in the garden a girl was working who looked like his daughter. There were three children playing around her. The girl said, "I'm glad to see you, father."

The peasant didn't know if she was his daughter but he said, "I would like my grandchildren to stay with me for a little while. Will you send them to me?"

And the girl answered, "Yes, I will."

The peasant travelled on and came to another house, and saw a girl who looked like his daughter working in the kitchen. And there were three children with her. This girl, too, greeted him as father and promised to let the grandchildren go to stay with him for a while.

The peasant travelled on and came to a third house, where a girl looked like his daughter and had three children. And she, too, promised to let the children stay with him.

After the peasant had returned home, the three girls who looked so much alike all brought their children to him and then went away. The peasant now had nine children in his house and he looked after them; but he also watched them to see how they behaved.

The three children of one girl never washed; their fingernails were dirty, they dropped things on the floor and left them there. And the peasant thought, "Now I know: these are the children of the girl who is not my daughter but who was a pig!"

The three children of the second girl could never sit still. They always jumped about and their hands were clumsy as if they had hooves on them! The peasant thought, "These are not my own grandchildren. These are the children of the girl who was a horse!"

But the three children of the third girl kept themselves clean and neat. They were quiet and well mannered and they could use their hands well. And the peasant said to himself, "These are the three children of my real daughter."

When the three girls came to fetch their children, the peasant went home with the girl who had the quiet, clean children and was his real daughter. And they lived together in her home.

The Dog with Two Masters

Once upon a time there was a man who earned his living by fishing. He had a dog — not a big dog but a small one who seemed all muscle. What do you call these dogs? Oh, yes: Jack Russells.

One day the fisherman was sitting on a stone and looking out to sea. The dog felt that his master was cross.

"What's the matter with you?"

"I can't go out to sea; it's too rough," answered the man.

"Oh, that!" said the dog. "Why do you always want to go out to sea? The land is so much better."

"Better, what do you mean, better? I can't make a living on land, can I?"

The dog didn't see why his master couldn't live on the land. *He* lived on the land! But his master got so annoyed that he said, "Get away from me or I'll drown you." The dog didn't like the sound of that word so he ran away quickly.

Then he came upon another man who was also sitting on a stone. "Why are men always sitting on stones? I mean, they're uncomfortable, they're hard!" He couldn't be doing with sitting on stones. Grass was much softer, or the earth if there was no grass, and then there were smells everywhere.

"What's the matter with you?" said the dog.

"Oh, I've had such a fight with my wife that I think I'll drown myself," answered the man.

The dog thought he couldn't understand this drowning business and sitting on stones, when there was a whole world full of lovely smells to explore.

"Why don't you take me and give me to your wife? She'll be so pleased, and she can take me for long walks."

"That's not a bad idea," said the man.

And together they went to the wife, who was so pleased to see her husband again *and* the little dog that she forgot all about the row she had had with her man.

But one day soon after, they met the first master of the dog.

"Hey, that's my dog!" he cried.

"No, I'm not," said the dog. "You wanted to drown me."

"I'm sorry, I was so upset about not being able to go out fishing. Of course I would never drown you; you have been my faithful friend ever since you were born. So please come back with me."

Now the dog was in a quandary: he also liked his new owners. And the wife had become very fond of him (and gave him lovely bones).

"Why don't we share him?" she said.

"Share him?" The dog had never heard of such a thing! "How? Does my first master have my head and forepaws, and the second owner my head and tail? Impossible!"

Now the wife had a great idea: "Why not leave him with me when you go out to sea and collect him when you come home? You're practically passing our door!"

"Excellent!" said the fisherman. "I never liked leaving him alone when I went fishing. Let's do that!"

So saying, everyone was content, and the dog had two masters who loved him, instead of just one.

A Michaelmas Story

Once upon a time, long, long ago, there was a small town with a wall all around it. The people lived happily there. At evening they closed the gates and in the morning they opened them again.

Imagine their surprise when they woke up one morning, looked over the wall, and what did they see? A dragon outside their gates! It wasn't a small dragon, no! It was a big dragon; it was a huge dragon.

Have you ever seen a dragon?

Well, I'll tell you what this one looked like: it had scales all over its body like a fish but very, very hard. It had a long swishy tail and from its mouth came fire and smoke.

"Don't open the gate this morning," said the people behind the wall. "We don't want a dragon in our town!" But they watched him over the wall, for they were curious what he would do.

Well, first he started to eat the grass but, of course, that was not enough for a dragon, so he started on the flowers and bushes.

At night-time he found a hole in the mountain and went to sleep there. The people of the town kept their eye on him. They could see he was still there, for there was fire and smoke coming out of the hole in the mountain.

Next morning out came the dragon again, looking as fierce as ever. As he had already eaten all the grass, the flowers and the bushes, he started on the trees. How awful it began to look outside the town. It was all bare! Then he got thirsty and he drank and drank until the river was empty.

When there was nothing left to eat or drink, he began to crawl towards the town. The people, who had never stopped watching him, became quite anxious. What was he going to eat next? Would he like the taste of people perhaps?

Well, when he got to the gate he started to make a terrible din. He swished his tail, he ground his teeth, he stamped his four big feet and he blew lots of fire and smoke into the air. It was very frightening and the people did not know what to do. All that day the dragon went round and round the town making more and more noise. At night he went back to his hole in the mountain, but he couldn't sleep as he was so hungry.

That night the people held a meeting. They asked the wisest man in the town for advice. His name was St Michael because he was a holy man. The people begged St Michael, who was not afraid of anything, to go out and slay the dragon with his sword. St Michael said that he would go out and meet the dragon the next morning.

And he DID!!

All the people in the town, young and old, rich and poor, were standing or sitting on the wall watching him. On he went, St Michael with his shining sword. They could see that he had reached the mountain now.

Oh, out came the dragon. St Michael held his sword up high and the dragon did not harm him. No, he lay down and looked up at St Michael sadly. St Michael spoke: "Do you know, dear dragon, that you are frightening the people of this town?"

"Frightening?" answered the dragon. "Why?"

"Well, your noise, your swishing of tail, your stamping of feet, but most of all your smoke and fire."

"But," said the dragon, "all dragons breathe smoke and fire. That is how they breathe and, you see. I am terribly lonely and I would so like to play with the children."

St Michael was astonished. "Is this really true? Play with the children? They think you're going to eat them!"

"Yes," said the dragon, "it is really true, I promise you," and he licked St Michael's hand to show he was telling the truth.

"Well," said St Michael, "we'll see if the people will let their children play with you, and if the children want to play with you." And so St Michael and the dragon walked towards the town together, St Michael in front and the dragon behind.

The people who were watching could hardly believe their eyes! But when they heard what St Michael had to tell them they could not believe their ears!

Now, there was a small girl who was always very brave, and she said, "I'll come and play with you".

"No! No!" shouted her parents, but she had already slipped through the gate, and the small, brave girl went out to meet the dragon. When she came near, she gave him a great big smile.

"Come here," she said. He came.

"Why don't you climb on my back and I'll give you a ride?"

St Michael lifted her up. How hard and sore the scales were. "Here," said St Michael, "take my cloak to sit on." And off she went, hanging on to his ears. It was great fun.

Soon a second child came out then a third, all wanting rides.

"Me next ..."

"Can I ...?"

"My turn ..."

In the end, almost all the children, except the shyest and the smallest, had a ride, and the poor dragon got so tired that he had to lie down.

Then the same little girl who had been so brave said, "Let's give him something to eat." And they all ran home and soon came back with leftover porridge, apples, old rolls, herrings and pancakes, and the dragon ate everything, even some old boots. And he felt so happy that he cried big dragon tears, and from that time onwards he became the pet of the town and everybody just loved him.

But do you know who the dragon loved most? St Michael, of course.

Three's Company

There were three of them: two girls and the dog, of course. The eldest girl was holding the dog's lead. The younger one, the inquisitive, enthusiastic type, was bounding ahead towards the sign. Willie Mills, the harbourmaster, had done his job well. The forecast had been poor and the weather was worsening. With the tide coming in, the seas would soon be breaking over the harbour wall to the east.

DANGER! PIER CLOSED,
BY ORDER OF THE HARBOURMASTER

The elder girl read the notice from a distance, standing still, the dog straining on the leash. The young one had to come right up to the board; as if not believing it, she had to actually touch it. And still she didn't want to accept it until the spray of the first load of water breaking on the wall touched her. She gave a shrill cry of surprise. And still she was about to defy it, had her sister not rushed up to restrain her. There was a short discussion and the three turned round.

The sea gained in strength and, at a safe distance, they clambered on the wall. It was very exciting lying there feeling the smash of the waves making the stones tremble. The waves came pounding in rhythmically. There were the usual seven or eight moderate ones and then a giant. It was fascinating to see them rolling along the wall, licking the stones, getting higher and higher, and then by some inexplicable law — maybe a rock underneath — breaking furiously, throwing spray all around. It is so mesmerising that many people can stand there quite still, following this spectacle developing, again and again. What power! What beauty! A shudder of fear can easily run over you.

The three moved farther away from the furore with each incoming wave. The older girl kept a tight hold of the dog, which moved around

148

the two, not wanting to miss anything. Every now and again, he jumped right between them, making sure he was one of the pack.

And then it happened. On one of these jumps he missed his footing and, yelping, fell over the side. It was so sudden that the falling dog pulled the lead from the girl's grasp. There was quite a spell between waves, and the dog wisely began swimming towards the shore.

The young girl, without hesitation, took off her shoes and coat and clambered down towards the place where she might catch the dog. At the first big wave, she was knocked over and lifted miraculously next to her furry friend.

Quite soon a small crowd had gathered to watch and were gesticulating and shouting advice. It was impossible to bring a boat around that corner as it was too rocky. The dog was sucked backwards and forwards by the surf and was beginning to lose strength. The girl, though, was very determined and tried to get at the dog despite the pull of the undertow.

Then the elder girl acted. She had said nothing, nor shouted nor waved her arms about. Her face was taut and pale. Her eyes were anxious. Suddenly she made a move. Instead of jumping in after the two, which she saw was useless and would only put her life in danger too, she grabbed a lifebelt that always hung on the wall near that spot for just such occasions. She ran round the wall on to the small stony beach. With a surprisingly accurate aim she threw the ring towards her sister, who was losing strength and very cold now.

In a moment she had caught it, and with the help of onlookers, she was pulled in, but looking back desperately to where she last saw the dog. He was very feeble now, having taken in a lot of water. His strength was ebbing. He seemed to be under water longer than above, and just thrusting out any old way against the waves.

Now there was quite a large crowd and they were determined to make a second rescue. Some youths made a chain by holding hands and one waded in, held by the others, until he was in the area where the dog was last seen.

"There he is!" they shouted — a pathetic black parcel totally at the mercy of the cold sea. They managed to pick him up and carry him up the stony beach. He lay quite still.

Then the elder girl ran towards him, calling his name. There was a faint trembling of the tail. She lifted him up and moved his chest. A great gulf of water came out of him. She called and called and held him close against her, cuddling him to the warmth of her body. His eyes opened for a moment.

Soon, all three were inside the house by the harbour in front of a roaring fire, the girls with hot drinks, the dog drying and sleeping off the ordeal.

Acknowledgments

My thanks go to Dora Kovacs for permission to use her late husband's stories, *The Harp with Five Strings*, *The Story of Ten Fingers*, *The Twelve Months*, and *A Tale of Nine Children*.

My thanks go to all Steiner kindergarten teachers who, over the years, have built up a wealth of stories and songs that have become traditional.

A huge thank you to my dear husband James who gave his time so freely in typing and editing, and who supported me throughout.

I have tried my best to contact the copyright holders of each story. If I have missed any acknowledgments, I am deeply sorry. I would like to thank all the writers mentioned below for creating such wonderful stories, which I've had the pleasure of sharing with so many children.

The poem 'One Day When we Went Walking' by Valine Hobbs is taken from *The Horn Book Magazine*, 1947.

Many of the stories are traditional folk tales, whose origins are now unknown: *The Little Jug*, *The Mitten*, *The Pearl-grey Cockerel*, *The Easter Hare*, *The Star Child*, *The Little Star's Search* (English), *How the Snowdrop Got its Colour*, *Hendrika's Adventure* (Dutch), *The Story of Beth*, *Erwin the Elf*, *King of the Birds* (Gaelic), *The Square Box* (Russian), *Long-legs* (Irish), *The Five Goats*.

The Tomten has been retold from a story by Astrid Lindgren, based on a poem by Viktor Rydberg.

Miaula and the Twins has been translated and retold from a Dutch story by Nienke van Hichtum.

Giant Grummer's Christmas has been retold from a story by William Dana Street, *The Tall Book of Christmas*, Harper and Brothers (1950).

Ameliaranne and the Green Umbrella has been retold from a story by Constance Heward (1920).

Joanna and the Jumble Sale has been retold from the story *Ameliaranne and the Jumble Sale* by Eileen Osborne (1943).

Bad Mousie has been retold from a story by Martha Ward Dudley, *The Tall Book of Make Believe*, Harper and Brothers (1950).

Susanna's Bears has been retold from a story by Mildred Lawrence, *The Tall Book of Make Believe*, Harper and Brothers (1950).

Several of the stories are retold from tales by the brothers Grimm: *The Seven Ravens, A Tale of Two Children (Jorinda and Jorindel), King Grizzly Beard, Hans in Luck*.

The Lion and the Mouse is based an Aesop's Fable.

Borka has been retold from a picture book by John Burningham, *Borka: The Adventures of a Goose with No Feathers*, Jonathan Cape Ltd (1963).

Granny Glittens and her Amazing Mittens has been retold from a story by Gertrude Crampton, *The Tall Book of Christmas*, Harper and Brothers (1950).

Some of the stories are retold from Rudyard Kipling's *Just So Stories: How the Zebra Got its Stripes, How the Elephant Got its Trunk, The Cat Who Walked Alone*.

Long-nose the Dwarf has been retold from a German fairy tale by Wilhelm Hauff.

And some of the stories are my own: *A Farm Story, Lassie, The Dog with Two Masters, A Michaelmas Story, Three's Company*.